Newcomer's Guide to Georgia

Newcomer's Guide to Georgia

by Don O'Briant

JOHN F. BLAIR
PUBLISHER   *Winston-Salem, North Carolina*

OPPOSITE TOP: *Six Flags over Georgia* / OPPOSITE BOTTOM: *Fountain in Forsyth Park, Savannah*
ABOVE: *Georgia's official fruit—the peach*
GEORGIA DEPARTMENT OF ECONOMIC DEVELOPMENT

JOHN F. BLAIR
PUBLISHER
1406 Plaza Drive
Winston-Salem, North Carolina 27103
www.blairpub.com

Manufactured in the United States of America

COVER IMAGES
FRONT COVER
Top row left to right: *Jekyll Island Beach; Forsyth Park in Savannah; Atlanta skyline*
Second row: *Tree-lined road in Thomasville*
Third row: *Peaches; Antebellum mansion in Savannah; Uga, the University of Georgia mascot*
Bottom row: *Callaway Gardens*

BACK COVER
Stone Mountain

CREDITS
PHOTOGRAPH OF UGA: ASHLEY CONNELL/UNIVERSITY OF GEORGIA ATHLETIC ASSOCIATION
ALL OTHER COVER IMAGES COURTESY OF GEORGIA DEPARTMENT OF ECONOMIC DEVELOPMENT

BOOK DESIGN BY DEBRA LONG HAMPTON

Library of Congress Cataloging-in-Publication Data

O'Briant, Don, 1943–
    Newcomer's guide to Georgia / by Don O'Briant.
        p.   cm.
    Includes bibliographical references and index.
    ISBN 978-0-89587-361-3 (alk. paper)
  1. Georgia—Guidebooks.   I.   Title.

  F284.3.O24   2009
  975.8'044—dc22
      2008051033

www.blairpub.com

OPPOSITE TOP: *Dogwood blossoms*
OPPOSITE BOTTOM: *Atlanta's Centennial Park*
GEORGIA DEPARTMENT OF ECONOMIC DEVELOPMENT

To all Georgians, past, present, and future

ABOVE: *Peach trees in bloom* / *The Georgia Dome*
OPPOSITE TOP: *Stone Mountain Park* / *Golfing*
GEORGIA DEPARTMENT OF ECONOMIC DEVELOPMENT

ABOVE: *Atlanta skyline at night*
OPPOSITE: *Mt. Yonah*
GEORGIA DEPARTMENT OF ECONOMIC DEVELOPMENT

Contents

Acknowledgments

Sailing on St. Simons
GEORGIA DEPARTMENT OF ECONOMIC
DEVELOPMENT

Bluegrass Festival
GEORGIA DEPARTMENT OF ECONOMIC DEVELOPMENT

Turnin & Burnin Pottery Festival in Gillsville
GEORGIA DEPARTMENT OF ECONOMIC DEVELOPMENT

Cumberland Island
GEORGIA DEPARTMENT OF ECONOMIC DEVELOPMENT

Acknowledgments

I wish to thank the staffs of the Georgia Department of Economic Development's Tourism Division, the Georgia Archives Department, and the Georgia Music Hall of Fame for their help and guidance.

Who We Are

Atlanta downtown lunch concert
GEORGIA DEPARTMENT OF ECONOMIC DEVELOPMENT

Welcome to Georgia.

If you are thinking of moving here or have already relocated, you can take comfort in knowing you are not alone. An estimated 30 percent of the state's 9,544,750 population was born elsewhere.

Georgia is the fastest-growing state in the South, according to the latest census figures. From 2000 to 2006, Georgia gained 228,415 people from outside the United States and 378,258 people from within the country.

In other words, Georgia has a diverse population that is getting more diverse. While some may complain about the influx of "foreigners," the addition of people of other nationalities, other races, and other skills is in general a good thing. After all, the people who founded the colony of Georgia in 1732 were a pretty diverse group. Although they came from England under the leadership of General James Edward Oglethorpe, they were English, Scots-Irish, Italians, Moravians, Sephardic Jews, Salzburgers, and Swiss.

Macon Cherry Blossom Festival
GEORGIA DEPARTMENT OF ECONOMIC DEVELOPMENT

Slaves who were brought here from Africa would add their own culture to the melting pot.

Today, Georgia's culture is a blend of Native American, African, and Scots-Irish cultures. Georgians generally are highly religious and mostly Christian. Seventy-six percent are Protestants, and eight percent are Catholics. Nearly 13 percent say they have no religion, and 2 percent have a religion other than Christianity.

According to 2006 statistics, 59 percent of the population is white, 29.8 percent is black or African-American, 7.1 percent is Hispanic or Latino, 2.7 percent is Asian, and 1.4 percent is from other or mixed races. The state is almost equally divided between the genders, with 50.5 percent of the population male and 49.5 percent female. Seventy-eight percent of Georgians are high-school graduates, and nearly a quarter of these have a bachelor's degree or higher.

Like other states below the Mason-Dixon line, Georgia is known for its Southern hospitality. That's not to say you won't encounter someone rude on the expressways of Atlanta, in a long line at the post office, or waiting at the Department of Motor Vehicles. Even the most polite Georgian has his or her limits. Furthermore, you can't be sure that the person criticizing your driving on I-85 by flashing a rude hand gesture is a true Georgian. He may be a newcomer or a tourist from another state where drivers actually obey the speed limits and signal when they change lanes.

Politicians used to say, "There's Atlanta, and then there's the rest of the state." That's still true to a certain extent, but Atlanta is changing, as are other cities and small towns in Georgia. No longer the "big small town" of the 1950s and early 1960s, Atlanta has acquired many of the perks—as well as the problems—of Northern urban centers.

Yes, we have professional sports teams, a nationally recognized symphony orchestra, live theater, art museums, a vibrant music scene, a busy international airport, and a booming economy. We also have traffic gridlock and other problems associated with rapid growth.

So if you're moving to Atlanta from a big city, you probably will adjust fairly quickly. If you're moving from a small town, remember to stay calm when you find yourself in bumper-to-bumper rush-hour traffic.

But Atlanta is just part of Georgia. Many suburbanites have nearly everything they need in their neighborhoods and venture into Atlanta only for ball games and special occasions. Some Georgians live happily in rural areas near medium-sized towns. Others would not think of living anywhere but the mountains or the coast.

One of the best things about Georgia is its geographic diversity. Even if you're stuck in the city because of your job, you can still escape on the weekends to balmy beaches on the Golden Isles and whitewater rivers in the mountains.

Media-Made Georgia

How outsiders view Georgia has been influenced greatly by the books, movies, and television shows about the people in the state. Some in other parts of the country—and other countries—still believe the spirit of Scarlett O'Hara is alive and well and living in Tara. Others who have seen the movie *Deliverance*, based on James Dickey's novel, are convinced that perverted and inbred hillbillies stalk unwary city folks who take canoe trips down the Chattooga River.

The television show and movie *The Dukes of Hazzard* reinforced the stereotypical image some have of the state as a land of good ole boys, fast cars, bumbling sheriffs, and overweight political kingpins. On the other hand, shows such as *In the Heat of the Night* and *I'll Fly Away* have painted a realistic portrait of racial relations in Georgia and the South.

To get an accurate picture of Georgia culture, read the literary works, listen to the music, and admire the art produced by Georgia's native sons and daughters. *Gone With the Wind*, Margaret Mitchell's novel, is very different from, and more realistic than, the movie in its portrayal of the Old South and the changes the Civil War brought. Flannery O'Connor's stories about eccentric characters in the South contain keen insights into the influence of religion on their lives. Erskine Caldwell's characters in *Tobacco Road* and *God's Little Acre* may seem stereotypical, but his message about poverty in the South was painfully true. Alice Walker's description of black rural life in Georgia in her Pulitzer Prize–winning novel *The Color Purple* offers a different perspective from Atlanta playwright Alfred Uhry's story of an affluent white Jewish woman and her black chauffeur in *Driving Miss Daisy*. And contemporary writers such as Terry Kay (*To Dance With the White Dog*), Anne Rivers Siddons (*Peachtree Road*), Paul Hemphill (*Long Gone*), Harry Crews (*A Feast of Snakes*), Mary Hood (*Familiar Heat*), and Pearl Cleage (*I Wish I Had a Red Dress*) have written eloquently about their personal literary landscapes.

Georgia's diversity is reflected most strikingly in its music, which ranges from country and folk to rock-'n'-roll and hip-hop. This is the state that produced James Brown and Fiddlin' John Carson, Little Richard and Travis Tritt, Ray Charles and R.E.M., Otis Redding and Usher.

Some of Georgia's early music, mainly in McIntosh County on the coast, included religious "shape note" singing and the "ring shout" of African-Americans, which involved a circular dance with clapping, stick beating, and call-and-response vocals. "Sacred Harp," or shape note music, is a technique that uses the shapes of notes to help the performance of singers who cannot sight-read music. The first Sacred Harp book was published in 1844 by Benjamin Franklin White and Elisha J. King of Georgia.

Atlanta has become a center for rap and hip-hop, including performers such as OutKast, TLC, Ludacris, Jermaine Dupri, L.A. Reid, and Lil John.

Other musical greats from Georgia include opera singer Jessye Norman; the late Robert Shaw, musical director of the Atlanta Symphony Orchestra, and Gladys Knight, whose biggest hit was "Midnight Train to Georgia."

You can learn more about the state's musicians in the "Arts and Entertainment" chapter and by visiting the Georgia Music Hall of Fame in Macon.

Famous Georgians

The list of people from Georgia who have made their mark in history or excelled in their professions is long and impressive.

The Reverend Martin Luther King, Jr., who preached nonviolence as he led the civil-rights movement that changed the country, was born in Atlanta and preached at Ebenezer Baptist Church.

Jimmy Carter, a peanut farmer from Plains, stunned political experts when he won the presidential election in 1976. As an ex-president, he has continued his work for global human rights through the Carter Center in Atlanta.

Ralph McGill, the Pulitzer Prize–winning editor of the *Atlanta Constitution*, gently—and sometimes not so gently—reminded Georgians that blacks were entitled to the same rights as whites and that racial and religious hatred should not be tolerated.

Jackie Robinson, who broke the color barrier in major league baseball with the Brooklyn Dodgers, was born in Cairo.

Henry "Hank" Aaron, another baseball great, broke Babe Ruth's career home run record while playing with the Atlanta Braves.

Margaret Mitchell, a reporter for the *Atlanta Journal*'s Sunday magazine, wrote only one book, but *Gone With the Wind* is a worldwide bestseller considered by millions of readers to be the classic love story.

Ted Turner, who revolutionized the media industry with CNN in Atlanta, still lives part-time near the television studio when he's not pursuing global peace and environmental protection.

Jane Fonda, the Oscar-winning actress who gave up her career for a decade to marry Ted Turner, remained in Atlanta after the divorce and is active in a group that seeks to prevent teen pregnancies.

Zell Miller, a former United States senator and governor, was instrumental in establishing the HOPE scholarship program, which pays state college tuition and fees for any Georgia high-school student who graduates with a B average or higher.

Humorists Jeff Foxworthy of "You Might Be a Redneck" fame; Roy Blount, Jr., author and a regular on *A Prairie Home Companion*; and late columnist and author Lewis Grizzard all grew up in Georgia.

Actress Julia Roberts, the star of *Steel Magnolias* and *Pretty Woman*, is from Smyrna. So is her brother, actor Eric Roberts. Georgia has sent a number of its other native sons and daughters to Broadway and Hollywood. Joanne Woodward of Thomasville is an Oscar-winning actress and wife of the late Paul Newman. Burt Reynolds of Waycross gave one of his best performances in the film *Deliverance*, which was shot in North Georgia. Dakota Fanning of Conyers is a rising child star who has appeared in films with Denzel Washington, Robert DeNiro, and Tom Cruise. The late Oliver Hardy, the larger half of the comedy film act Laurel and Hardy, was born in Harlem, near Augusta. The late Melvyn Douglas of Macon is perhaps best known for his role in *Hud* opposite Paul Newman. Other stars from the state include

Ossie Davis, Kim Basinger, Lawrence Fishburne, Miriam Hopkins, and Stacy Keach.

In politics, Georgia has produced not only a United States president but United States Supreme Court justice Clarence Thomas, United Nations ambassador Andrew Young, Attorney General Griffin Bell, and Secretary of State Dean Rusk. Atlanta made history when it elected Maynard Jackson as the first black mayor and Shirley Franklin as the first black woman mayor of a major Southern city.

In sports, former University of Georgia football coach Vince Dooley and Bobby Dodd, the late Georgia Tech coach, are considered legends by their teams' fans. The state's outstanding athletes include football greats Herschel Walker and Jim Brown, NASCAR star Bill Elliott, golf champion Bobby Jones, baseball Hall of Famer Ty Cobb, and boxing champions Larry Holmes and Evander Holyfield.

Other famous Georgians include songwriter Johnny Mercer, who composed "Moon River" and many other hit songs; Joel Chandler Harris, author of the Uncle Remus tales; Carson McCullers, author of *The Heart Is a Lonely Hunter*; artist Jasper Johns; blues pioneer Blind Willie McTell; Wild West hero John Henry "Doc" Holliday; Big Band leader Harry James; and Girl Scouts founder Juliette Gordon Low.

Talking the Talk

The ways we speak in different parts of the state are as diverse as Georgia's geography.

In Atlanta, for instance, you can go for days without hearing a Southern accent because of the large numbers of Northerners and Midwesterners who have moved here.

Head to rural South Georgia or the coast and you'll hear different subdialects of Southern American English. Former president Jimmy Carter's South Georgia accent is different from former governor Zell Miller's Appalachian accent. The "cracker" dialect is heard mostly in South Georgia. Many people in North Georgia speak with a southern Appalachian accent. And not everybody talks like comedian Jeff Foxworthy.

In Savannah, Atlanta, and other parts of the state, you'll hear a refined version of the Southern accent that makes words flow out as slowly as honey on a cold day. On the coast, you might hear the Gullah or Geechee dialect spoken by African-Americans on the barrier islands.

State Botanical Garden of Georgia
GEORGIA DEPARTMENT OF ECONOMIC DEVELOPMENT

Yes, we do say "y'all" a lot, but remember that y'all is plural. Don't embarrass yourself with native Georgians by saying, "Y'all come back now," if you are saying goodbye to an individual. And always remember to respond correctly when a Georgian asks, "How's your mama'nem?" Translated, it means, "How are your mother and the rest of the family?"

Outsiders have poked fun at the way the mountain people talk, but the language of Appalachia actually can be traced back to Elizabethan England during the time a reasonably adept wordsmith named Shakespeare was writing a few plays. In Zell Miller's memoir, *The Mountains Within Me*, the former governor and United States senator explains how some mountain terms are the same ones used in England hundreds of years ago. Mountaineers might say "betwixt" instead of "between," "nary" instead of "neither," "puny" instead of "sickly," "bar" for "bear," and "cheer" for "chair."

Miller notes that mountain people are also apt to use colorful expressions, many of which have become part of universal usage:

> Purty as a speckled pup under a red wagon.
> Rough as a cob.
> Rode hard and put up wet.
> Borned tired and raised lazy.
> All tuckered out.

If you stay long enough in Georgia, you'll hear more of these expressions and maybe invent a few of your own. Meanwhile, relax and enjoy the rest of the book. In the following chapters, I'll introduce you to the people and places of

Georgia, tell a little about its history and landscape, and offer the information you need to know about getting a driver's license and auto insurance, paying taxes, and finding a college.

I'll also tell you about our economy, our sports, our arts and crafts, our natural wonders, and the kinds of food and beverages we consume. I'll try to give you all the information you need to become a Georgian, or at least to act enough like one to fool the natives.

BOOKS AND RESOURCES

Grizzard, Lewis. *If I Ever Get Back to Georgia, I'm Gonna Nail My Feet to the Ground.* New York: Villard Books, 1990.

Kirby, Jack Temple. *Media-Made Dixie: The South in the American Imagination.* Athens: University of Georgia Press, 1986.

Miller, Zell. *The Mountains Within Me.* Atlanta, Ga.: Cherokee Press, 1985.

New Georgia Encyclopedia. www.georgiaencyclopedia.org.

The Land

Mountain farm in Trenton
GEORGIA DEPARTMENT OF ECONOMIC DEVELOPMENT

Georgia is known as "the Empire State of the South" for good reason. With an area of 58,930 square miles, it's the largest state east of the Mississippi River. Geographically, the state is divided into five diverse regions: the Appalachian Plateau, in a tiny northwestern corner; the Ridge and Valley Region, also in the northwest; the Blue Ridge in northeastern Georgia; the Piedmont; and the Atlantic Coastal Plain.

The Appalachian Plateau in Dade County is part of a plateau that begins in New York and ends in Alabama. The adjoining Ridge and Valley Region is the source of much of the coal mined in the United States. As the home of Cloudland Canyon State Park, this area offers some of the state's most scenic views.

The Blue Ridge gets its name from the blue haze that often surrounds the mountains. The highest peak in the Blue Ridge is Brasstown Bald in Towns County, at 4,796 feet. Rabun Bald in Rabun County and Tray Mountain in Towns and White counties are slightly lower, at 4,694 feet and 4,430 feet,

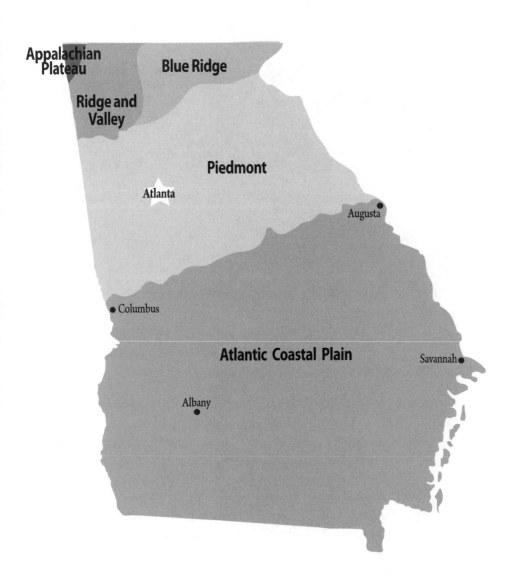

Appalachian
Plateau

Blue Ridge

Ridge and
Valley

Piedmont

Atlanta

Augusta

Columbus

Atlantic Coastal Plain

Savannah

Albany

respectively. The Appalachian Trail begins—or ends, depending on where you start—at Springer Mountain, a 3,782-foot peak in Gilmer County. Hikers on the trail face a higher challenge in Union County on Blood Mountain, which measures 4,461 feet.

The Eastern Continental Divide follows the crest of the Blue Ridge Mountains. It serves as the dividing line between rivers and streams that drain into the Gulf of Mexico and those that drain into the Atlantic Ocean. Much of the land in this area is part of the 750,000-acre Chattahoochee National Forest, home to hardwoods, evergreens, rushing mountain streams, pristine lakes, and tumbling waterfalls. Amicalola Falls is the tallest waterfall east of the Mississippi. Other scenic waterfalls include Anna Ruby, Toccoa, and Hiawassee.

Among the rivers in the region, the wild and scenic Chattooga is the most popular among kayakers, canoeists, and whitewater rafters. The Chattooga was made famous—or infamous, depending on your point of view—by James Dickey's novel *Deliverance* and the subsequent movie starring Burt Reynolds, Jon Voight, and Ned Beatty.

The Piedmont, south of the Blue Ridge, is an area of gently rolling hills. The state's most populous cities—Atlanta, Augusta, Athens, Columbus, and Macon—are in the Piedmont. Geographic landmarks include the Savannah River in the east, Lake Lanier in the north, and the Chattahoochee River, which flows through the Piedmont and Atlanta on its way to the Gulf of Mexico. One of the most unusual landmarks is Stone Mountain, a 1,683-foot peak of exposed granite 16 miles from Atlanta.

The Piedmont is separated from the Atlantic Coastal Plain by the fall line, a narrow strip that marks the end of the crystalline rocks of the Piedmont and the sedimentary rocks of what was the coastline millions of years ago.

Georgia's Coastal Plain includes the Upper Coastal Plain and the Lower Coastal Plain. Both are prime agricultural areas for peanuts, soybeans, cotton, tobacco, pecans, and peaches. Antebellum plantations thrived along the middle and most fertile region, known as the Black Belt. The soil becomes sandier and less desirable for growing crops the closer you get to the coast. Many farms in this area have been turned into pine forests and sold to pulpwood and lumber companies.

If you keep driving south through the Coastal Plain, you will eventually run into the Okefenokee Swamp, the nation's largest wildlife refuge. The Okefenokee—"Land of the Trembling Earth" in Seminole—was created when the eastern ridge rose abruptly, isolating a vast pocket of coastal water. Vegetation and cypress trees gradually spread until the area became one gigantic peat bog.

That's what scientists say. The Seminoles have a more interesting explanation for how the Okefenokee was formed. According to legend, the swamp was created when humans fought beavers over ownership of the land. The beavers, who were poor losers, broke all of their dams, flooded the area, and then left. To this day, the Okefenokee is full of wildlife and waterfowl—but no beavers. The Suwannee River, made famous in Stephen Foster's song, originates in the Okefenokee.

If you head west toward Columbus, you'll encounter Providence Canyon. Described as "Georgia's Little Grand Canyon," Providence has colorful red-and-white walls that descend sharply from a forested area dotted with rare wildflowers.

Georgia's Lower Coastal Plain includes the Atlantic coast and the barrier islands. Geologists have found a series of prehistoric terraces—former coastlines—formed by rising and falling sea levels during the Ice Age. The coastline is still changing today, thanks to waves, wind, currents, and tides.

This region is famous for the historic port of Savannah and 100 miles of beaches, marshlands, and barrier islands including St. Simons, Jekyll, Sea Island, and Tybee. While these islands have become popular resort destinations, Cumberland Island is protected by the National Park Service. Wild horses still run free on Cumberland, and loggerhead turtles lay their eggs on the beach.

Providence Canyon
GEORGIA DEPARTMENT OF ECONOMIC DEVELOPMENT

Cumberland Island sand dunes and beach
GEORGIA DEPARTMENT OF ECONOMIC DEVELOPMENT

Other barrier islands are Little Tybee, Ossabaw, Wassaw, St. Catherines, Sapelo, Wolf, Blackbeard, Little St. Simons, and Little Cumberland. Sea Island, Jekyll, St. Simons, and Tybee are accessible by bridges, but other islands can be reached only by boat.

Hundreds of years ago, Native Americans farmed and fished on these islands. The Spanish, who established a mission during the 1500s, grew figs, peaches, and citrus crops. Later, plantation owners cultivated rice, sea-island cotton, and indigo. At the end of the 19th century and the beginning of the 20th century, Northern industrialists and millionaires bought some of the islands and turned them into resorts and private playgrounds for themselves and their friends.

Climate

There used to be a common saying in Georgia: "If you don't like the weather, don't worry, it'll change pretty soon." I'm not sure that's true anymore. For the last few years, North Georgia has been under a severe drought that has dropped lake levels drastically and led to outdoor watering restrictions for homeowners in several counties. Thunderstorms still pop up in the summer, but some parts of the state are 15 inches or more below the normal average amount of rainfall.

Newcomers to Georgia can expect to find very hot and humid weather from June through most of September. Yes, I know what the tourism and chamber of commerce folks say about the average temperature, but you can take those figures with a grain of salt—or a large tumbler of ice water or sweet tea.

The good news is that winters are relatively mild in most parts of the state. The mountain areas get a few snowfalls and an occasional ice storm, but that's nothing compared to what folks endure in Minnesota or Buffalo, New York.

The great news is that spring and fall are glorious in Georgia. The colors of the leaves in autumn make the landscape look like one giant quilt. And spring is a season of blooming azaleas, dogwoods, apple and peach trees, and uncountable flowers both wild and domestic.

Here, then, is a more detailed description of the weather you can expect from each region.

The climate in the northern, mountainous part of the state varies according to elevation. Summer temperatures generally average in the mid-80s, with a few days in the 90s. Winter temperatures frequently are below freezing, and snowfalls of several inches are not unusual. Annual average temperature in the mountains is in the 50s.

In the Piedmont, the average winter temperature is a little warmer—about 57 degrees—and the summer temperature is a lot warmer—about 89 degrees with high humidity. Snowfalls of one or two inches occur only once or twice a year but generally create massive traffic problems, especially in Atlanta.

You won't need many sweaters if you live in the Coastal Plain. This area has mild winters and few days below freezing. The annual average temperature is 77 degrees, which sounds ideal until you realize that summer temperatures in the high 90s are not uncommon. Rainfall is heaviest along the coast.

Georgia does occasionally have extreme weather. The lowest recorded temperature was 17 degrees below zero and the highest recorded temperature 112 degrees. Georgia is not as susceptible to tornadoes as the Midwest, but it has been hit by some severe storms. The most recent tornado hit downtown Atlanta on March 14, 2008, damaging the World Congress Center, the Georgia Dome, and several surrounding skyscrapers while thousands of spectators were in the dome watching the Southeastern Conference basketball tournament. No deaths were reported.

Hurricanes are not a major treat for direct hits on the coast, but tropical storms occasionally cause flooding and heavy rains and winds in the middle and southern parts of the state.

Cherry blossoms in Macon
GEORGIA DEPARTMENT OF ECONOMIC DEVELOPMENT

Flora

Georgia is still a relatively green state, despite the construction of office parks, shopping malls, and subdivisions. Some cities have enacted ordinances requiring approval by an arborist before certain kinds of trees can be cut.

Most of Georgia's 250 species of trees are grown for commercial purposes. These include pecan, white and yellow pine, white oak, cypress, cedar, hickory, and maple, as well as fruit trees such as peach, pear, and cherry. Other trees in the state are yellow poplar, sycamore, sweet gum, black gum, dogwood, sassafras, and magnolia.

Flowering shrubs include mountain laurel, rhododendron, flowering quince, and yellow jasmine. Spanish moss can be found hanging from live oaks in the Coastal Plain. And kudzu, a vine imported from Japan to control erosion, is rapidly taking over every abandoned barn and junked car in the state.

Georgia has 155 plant species on its protected and endangered lists. These include pink lady's-slipper, smooth purple coneflower, hummingbird flower, Alabama milkvine, Georgia indigo bush, nutmeg hickory, hairy rattleweed, leather flower, and American barberry. A complete list can be found at the Georgia Department of Natural Resources website, www.gadnr.org. A good

Basketmaking with kudzu vines
GEORGIA DEPARTMENT OF ECONOMIC DEVELOPMENT

Kudzu

This creepy, crawly, climbing vine from Japan was supposed to save Southern soil from eroding and washing away to the Atlantic Ocean and the Gulf of Mexico.

Introduced by the Japanese at the 1876 Philadelphia Centennial Exposition, it was not planted in Georgia until the 1920s. What began as an invasion of small cuttings spread like, well, kudzu during the 1930s, when the Soil Conservation Service enlisted the Civilian Conservation Corps to plant the vine to help control erosion. The government was so enthusiastic about kudzu that it paid farmers $8 an acre to plant it.

If kudzu had a spokesman, it was Channing Cope, a Covington radio host who wrote a farm column for the *Atlanta Journal-Constitution*. Cope even started the Kudzu Club. In 1949, he wrote the book *Front Page Farming*, in which he encouraged farmers to plant their entire acreage in kudzu as food for cows and other livestock.

Little did Cope and agricultural experts realize what they had unleashed. In his poem *Kudzu*, James Dickey likens it to a Japanese invasion and warns Georgians to keep their bedroom windows closed to prevent the vine from creeping inside while they sleep.

Dickey wasn't exaggerating much. The plant seemed to grow overnight, climbing trees and covering abandoned houses and barns. The United States Department of Agriculture finally recognized kudzu as a weed in 1972, but it was too late by that time. Kudzu had taken root in Southern culture, as well as in much of its unused farmland.

place to see many of Georgia's native plants is the 300-acre State Botanical Garden of Georgia in Athens. Classes are offered in the preservation of native plants and other gardening subjects.

Okefenokee Swamp Great Egret
GEORGIA DEPARTMENT OF
ECONOMIC DEVELOPMENT

Fauna

Although development and overhunting have thinned or eliminated some wildlife, Georgia is still home to more than 90 species of animals, including white-tailed deer, rabbits, opossums, raccoons, black bears, muskrats, minks, foxes, and squirrels.

Gone are the bison, red wolves, and wild cougars that roamed the forests and fields when the first Europeans arrived in the 1500s and 1600s. Species that have declined in number in Georgia's coastal waters include manatees, right whales, and humpbacks.

The animals that have survived and thrived are the ones most adaptable to their changing habitat. The raccoon population, for example, has increased in Georgia.

More than 130 bird species, including the brown thrasher (the state bird), the mockingbird, the bobwhite quail (the state game bird), and a variety of sparrows can be found in most places in the state. Other native birds are cardinals, ruby-throated hummingbirds, catbirds, wrens, owls, purple martins, whippoorwills (or goatsuckers), hawks, herons, buzzards, bald eagles, snowy egrets, and white ibises.

Georgia's diverse habitats are attractive to birds that stop and stay awhile before migrating to other places. At one time or another, some 347 species of birds can be seen in the state, particularly in the coastal areas.

Birds in Georgia can be classified as permanent residents, summer

Seagulls at St. Simons
GEORGIA DEPARTMENT OF
ECONOMIC DEVELOPMENT

breeders that migrate from Central and South America, winter residents, and Neotropical migrants that stop in Georgia in the spring and fall.

Mark Catesby, an ornithologist who arrived in Georgia in 1723, was the first to systematically count and list the birds in the state. John Bartram sighted 215 birds and noted them in his 1791 book, *Travels*. Later, famous artist John James Audubon included paintings of the birds he found in Georgia in *Birds of America*. Thomas Burleigh's 1958 book, *Georgia's Birds*, is considered the first comprehensive work on the state's feathered inhabitants.

Georgia is a great place for bird watching because of its location on the Eastern flyway migration route. More than 350 species, from woodpeckers to blue jays, can be seen throughout the year. One of the best places for bird watchers is Harris Neck National Wildlife Refuge in McIntosh County. Located on an abandoned World War II army airfield, the refuge consists of 2,700 acres of forests, open fields, and saltwater marshes. These different habitats support songbirds, birds of prey, wading birds, and waterfowl. Wood storks and white ibises can be seen most any season, but the best time to see great egrets, snowy egrets, black-crowned night herons, and other waders is in May and June. Painted buntings are most plentiful from late spring through summer.

The state has 42 species of snakes. While you may not like them, they provide a useful service by keeping the rodent population under control. Most snakes are harmless, but beware the following poisonous varieties found in most parts of the state: copperheads, water moccasins, Eastern diamondback rattlesnakes, and pigmy rattlesnakes. Coral snakes usually don't venture far from the Coastal Plain of Georgia. They are more common in Florida.

Georgia is a fisherman's paradise whether you're interested in mountain trout, largemouth bass, flounder, or mullet. The lakes of Georgia teem with catfish, bream, crappie, eel, and shad, while the coastal waters are alive with crabs, turtles, shrimp, oysters, mackerel, and other saltwater fish.

The state is one of the nation's leaders in the preservation of wildlife and wildlife habitat and was one of the first to pass legislation protecting tidal marshlands. Thousands of acres are protected in national forests. The Georgia Conservancy is also active in preserving natural areas.

Settlement and Environmental Issues

The geography of Georgia influenced how it was settled and what happened to the environment once more people arrived. The Native Americans who first came to what is now known as Georgia more than 10,000 years ago used fire as a tool to clear forests and create fields. Lightning strikes also played a role in burning some forests.

As the Native Americans became less nomadic, they tended to settle in the river valleys, where they built earthen mounds, permanent residences, and stockades. As they set fires to clear more land, different types of vegetation, such as cane, replaced the trees along the rivers and streams.

When the Europeans arrived, they quickly transformed the environment by cutting trees in large numbers, gathering ginseng, and trapping animals for their pelts. By the early 1700s, millions of deer hides and beaver, fox, otter, and elk skins were shipped to Europe. As animals such as buffalo, beaver, and elk became scarce or disappeared, agriculture began to replace trapping as a source of income. Rice plantations sprang up along the coast, and cotton farms were carved out of timberland in the rest of the state.

General James Oglethorpe prohibited the owning of slaves when he founded Georgia, but competition from slave-owning planters in South Carolina and protests from Georgia settlers soon forced him to lift the ban. The introduction of slaves in the 1750s sparked a growth in large plantations in the coastal area. Cotton production in the upcountry and the Piedmont boomed after the invention of Eli Whitney's cotton gin in 1793. Until then, cotton had to be separated from the seeds by hand. This was not difficult for the long-staple sea-island cotton but was very tedious for the short-staple upland cotton. The cotton gin allowed the expansion of cotton plantations and the addition of more slaves in the northern and western parts of the state.

As fields grew less fertile after repeated crops of cotton, farmers abandoned them to erosion and moved on to better soil. Left barren, the soil eroded into streams. Silt buildup in the streams resulted in flooding. The emancipation of the slaves after the Civil War reduced much of the cotton industry, but the heaviest damage came from the migration of the boll weevil into the Southern states in the 1920s.

Deforestation

Until the Civil War, most logging was done along rivers or large streams that allowed the logs to be floated to ports. The expansion of railroads and the use of portable sawmills after the war drastically changed Georgia's landscape.

Over the last three decades of the 19th century, timber companies decimated longleaf pine forests and the cypresses in the Okefenokee Swamp. By the 1930s, overcutting, urbanization, and the advent of the automobile drastically reduced much of Georgia's forests.

Two things helped reverse the trend in the late 1930s: new trees began sprouting on abandoned farmland, and Congress passed the Soil Conservation Act. Under the act, farmers were encouraged to turn some of their fields into pastures, to create terraces and plant kudzu to control erosion, and to practice strip cropping and plant rotation. These efforts, immediately successful, were boosted in 1944 when Congress passed the Flood Control Act to create dams and recreational lakes.

The landscape was changed again when University of Georgia chemist Charles Herty found a way to use young pines to make paper. Tree farming suddenly became more profitable, and much of the abandoned farmland was converted to pine plantations.

More recently, ecology activists such as Janisse Ray, author of *Ecology of a Cracker Childhood*, have campaigned for the preservation and replanting of longleaf pine forests, particularly in the wire-grass area of the state. Other conservation groups are also engaged in saving the forests and wetlands, and logging companies have reduced or eliminated the practice of clear-cutting.

Several divisions of the Georgia Department of Natural Resources have the missions of conservation and management of development.

The Coastal Resources Division is in charge of the preservation of natural, environmental, archaeological, historic, and recreational resources along the 11-county coastal region. It also monitors water quality.

The Fish and Wildlife Management Division is responsible for enforcing wildlife laws and protecting threatened and endangered species. Individual landowners can obtain help in managing wildlife on their property from this division.

In addition to overseeing state parks, the Parks, Recreation, and Historic Sites Division works to reduce invasive non-native plants so that native plants can benefit. It uses controlled burns to improve natural areas and allows quota hunts to control deer overpopulation.

Population and Pollution

Unfortunately, wherever you find people, you'll generally find pollution. With the population of Georgia more than doubling from 4 million in 1960 to over 9 million in 2006, pollution and diminishing water resources are greater problems than ever. A drought that has lasted several years in much of the state has created a major concern about water supplies as urban development continues at a rapid pace.

The water quality of the Chattahoochee River, which provides drinking water for half of all Georgians, continues to be threatened by urban sprawl, runoff from construction sites and farmland, and seepage from septic tanks. Metro Atlanta alone has more than a million septic tanks.

Urban sprawl has resulted in the destruction of some animal habitats and threatens the survival of some native plant species. The 1973 federal Endangered Species Act has helped, as has the 2000 Georgia Community Greenspace Program, created by the state legislature. The program encourages counties to preserve at least 20 percent of their land and water as green space. Counties that voluntarily do this are given extra funds.

Air quality is a major issue in metropolitan Atlanta. The city and neighboring counties have more than 16,000 miles of roads and the fourth-worst traffic congestion in the country. Besides outbursts of road rage by angry commuters, all that traffic produces high ozone levels. The poor air quality has led to an increase in respiratory illnesses, according to the Centers for Disease Control and Prevention.

Rivers and Lakes

Georgia has more than 12,000 miles of rivers and streams. These include the Altamaha, Chattahoochee, Chattooga, Conasauga, Coosa, Coosawattee,

Altamaha River
GEORGIA DEPARTMENT OF
ECONOMIC DEVELOPMENT

Etowah, Flint, Ochlockonee, Ocmulgee, Oconee, Ogeechee, Oostanaula, Satilla, Savannah, St. Marys, Suwannee, and Toccoa rivers.

North Georgia is home to a series of lakes created by the Georgia Power Company to produce electricity. The recreational pursuits available at the resulting reservoirs were a bonus.

The creation of Lake Burton in 1919 upset the residents of the village of Burton and other landowners because they had to sell their property and move. Today, the lake's shoreline is dotted with vacation homes.

Farther down the Tallulah River is the Nacoochee Hydroelectric Plant, which created Lake Seed when the dam was built in 1926. Lake Rabun was completed on the same river in 1915; its generating plant was added farther downstream because the force of the untamed river at Tallulah Falls was so much greater. The Native American name for this area was *Talula,* which means "the terrible." The construction of the power plant involved digging a tunnel through the mountain, separate crews starting on opposite sides and meeting in the middle. Fortunately, the calculations were accurate and the tunnels met with less than an inch of difference.

Covering 63 acres, Tallulah Lake is the smallest Georgia Power lake. When the accompanying hydroelectric plant was completed in 1913, it was the third largest in the United States in the production of kilowatts.

Georgia Power's dam creating Tugalo Lake on the Tugaloo River was completed in 1923, after construction was halted in 1917 following the outbreak of World War I. The Cherokee name *Tugalo* means "fork of a stream," apparently in reference to the Tallulah and Chattooga rivers' joining to form the Tugaloo. It is unknown why the name of the river is spelled differently from the name of the lake.

Lake Yonah is a Georgia Power lake on the Tugaloo River in northeastern

Georgia. The Yonah Hydroelectric Plant began operating in 1925. *Yonah* means "big black bear" in Cherokee.

Lake Trahlyta, a small lake in Vogel State Park, was named for a Cherokee maiden. The state park, however, was named for a German family that set up a tanning company in Milwaukee. The company bought land in North Georgia to acquire bark from hardwood trees to make tannin. The family later donated the land to Georgia for the park.

Where you have mountain streams, you'll frequently have waterfalls, and Georgia is home to some of the most picturesque. Anna Ruby Falls—twin falls that drop 150 feet and 50 feet to form Smith Creek—is located in the Chattahoochee National Forest. At 729 feet, Amicalola Falls in Dawsonville is the tallest cascading waterfall east of the Mississippi. *Amicalola* is the Cherokee word for "tumbling waters." Other scenic waterfalls in the state are Toccoa Falls, Panther Creek Falls, and DeSoto Falls.

Three large lakes have been created on the Savannah River, which forms Georgia's eastern border with South Carolina. Hartwell Dam, completed in 1963 by the Army Corps of Engineers, is located seven miles below where the Tugaloo and Seneca rivers join to form the Savannah. Hartwell Lake has a shoreline of 962 miles and extends 49 miles up the Tugaloo and 45 miles up the Seneca.

Richard B. Russell Dam and Lake are located 30 miles downstream from Hartwell Dam and 37 miles upstream from the J. Strom Thurmond Dam. The Army Corps of Engineers completed the project in 1983 for flood control, power production, and fish and wildlife management. Named for late United States senator Richard B. Russell of Georgia, Russell Lake covers 26,650 acres.

Clarks Hill/Thurmond Lake, another project of the Army Corps of Engineers, was built between 1946 and 1954. It is one of the 10 most visited lakes in the country. Created by Thurmond Dam (named after late United States senator Strom Thurmond of South Carolina), it is located on the Savannah River 22 miles above Augusta and 239.5 miles from the mouth of the Savannah. The 71,100-acre lake has a shoreline of 1,200 miles.

One of the most picturesque mountain lakes is Lake Blue Ridge. Formed in 1930 when the Toccoa Electric Power Company built the Blue Ridge Dam on the Toccoa River, the reservoir was purchased by the Tennessee Valley Authority in 1939.

Other lakes in North Georgia are Carters Lake on the Coosawattee River near Ellijay; Lake Allatoona, north of Marietta; Lake Acworth, about 30 miles north of Atlanta; and Lake Lanier, a main source of water for Atlanta. Named for poet Sidney Lanier, the 38,000-acre lake was created when Buford

Dam was constructed on the Chattahoochee River in 1956. It is also fed by the Chestatee River. The lake is a popular recreational area and location for second homes, but dropping water levels due to a lengthy drought have left many waterfront residences high and dry.

Located east of Atlanta near Greensboro and Eatonton, Lake Oconee was created in 1979 when the Georgia Power Company built Wallace Dam on the Oconee River. Lake Oconee is the second-largest lake in Georgia. Several upscale resort communities have been built at the lake, including Reynolds Plantation and the Ritz-Carlton Lodge. Just down the Oconee River from Lake Oconee is Lake Sinclair, a 15,330-acre lake created in 1953 to provide electricity and recreation for the Milledgeville area. Other lakes near Oconee and Sinclair are Tobesofkee Lake in Bibb County and Jackson Lake in Jasper, Newton, and Butts counties. One of the oldest man-made lakes in Georgia, the 4,750-acre Jackson Lake was created in 1910 when Lloyd Shoals Dam was built. The Yellow, Alcovy, and South rivers form Jackson Lake.

Located on the Georgia-Alabama border, West Point Lake is another Army Corps of Engineers lake. West Point has a shoreline of 535 miles and extends 35 miles along the Chattahoochee River.

Fed by the Chattahoochee and Flint rivers, Lake Seminole is a 37,500-acre lake along the Georgia-Florida border in the southwestern corner of the state.

Atlanta interstates
GEORGIA DEPARTMENT OF ECONOMIC DEVELOPMENT

Some State Statistics

Land area	57,906 square miles
Water	1,522 square miles
Total area	59,428 square miles
Persons per square mile	141.4
Bounded by	Tennessee, South Carolina, North Carolina, Florida, and Alabama

Athens
GEORGIA DEPARTMENT OF ECONOMIC DEVELOPMENT

Origins of Cities

Here is a list of Georgia cities with populations of at least 30,000 in the 2000 census.

Atlanta   The capital of Georgia, Atlanta was initially named Terminus in 1837, when engineers for the Western and Atlantic Railroad staked out a point—a zero milepost—that was to be the end of the line for the railroad they planned to build from Chattanooga, Tennessee. In 1843, the name was changed to Marthasville in honor of former governor Wilson Lumpkin's daughter. After more rail lines were built to converge in the town, the name was changed again in 1845, to Atlanta. The city's rapid growth in the 1800s was due to the fact that it was connected by rail to the rest of the state and the Southeast.

Augusta   Augusta is the second-oldest city in Georgia, after Savannah. Named for Princess Augusta of Saxe-Gotha, the wife of Frederick, Prince of Wales, Augusta began in 1736 as a trading center after Georgia founder James Oglethorpe reached an agreement with the Creek Indians. Augusta's location on the Savannah River was ideal for traders and later for industrial growth.

Columbus   Founded in 1828, Columbus became an industrial center in the 1800s because of its location on the Chattahoochee River at the fall line. The river proved an easy way to transport cotton and was later harnessed to provide power. The construction of water-powered gristmills, sawmills, and textile mills established Columbus as one of the first mill towns in the South.

Savannah   The oldest city in Georgia, Savannah was founded in 1733 by James Oglethorpe as a place for the first British colonists to begin their new lives. Oglethorpe designed Savannah on a London model of central squares. Savannah became the first capital of Georgia after the Revolutionary War and was one of the world's major cotton-shipping ports.

Athens   Athens is the result of a 1785 decision by the Georgia legislature to endow a college. In 1801, John Milledge, a future governor and member of the committee sent to find a site, purchased a parcel of 623 acres on the Oconee River and donated it to the trustees of the new university. The site was named Athens after the Greek center of culture, and the University of Georgia was born. Incorporated in 1806, Athens became a university town as well as a center for textile manufacturing.

Macon   The town of Macon was incorporated in 1823 on the banks of the Ocmulgee River. Lots in the town were laid out and put up for auction, and farmland was distributed by lottery. As cotton farmers brought their bales to Macon to be shipped down the Ocmulgee to Darien, the town prospered. Stores were built to sell goods to the farmers, and banks opened to take their money.

Sandy Springs   Located in Fulton County, Sandy Springs is a suburb of Atlanta that voted to incorporate as a city in 2005. The springs for which the town is named are a local historic site. The estimated population of Sandy Springs for 2006 was 85,771.

Roswell   The city of Roswell, northwest of Atlanta, began as a cotton mill established in the 1830s by Roswell King. The mill, which used slave labor, was the largest in North Georgia. King invited more coastal planters to start cotton plantations in the area, and mill production soon increased dramatically. So did the residents. In 1854, Roswell was incorporated as a city.

Albany   The county seat of Dougharty County was founded in 1836 by land speculator Nelson Tift. Located on the Flint River, Albany was a choice market site for cotton farmers. After the line from Savannah was completed in 1857, Albany soon became the rail center of southwestern Georgia.

Marietta   Founded as a chartered village in 1834, Marietta was named in honor of Mary Moore, the widow of United States senator Thomas W. Cobb. The completion of the Western and Atlantic Railroad to Atlanta and Chattanooga, Tennessee, spurred development and tourism. As increasing numbers of wealthy coastal residents spent their summers in Marietta for its

relatively mild climate and its spring water, more hotels and stores were built. Marietta officially became a town with a mayor and a council in 1852.

Valdosta The county seat of Lowndes County, Valdosta was incorporated in 1860 at a site about 20 miles from the Florida line. Troupville was the county seat until the Atlantic and Gulf Railroad built its tracks four miles south of the town. Lowndes County residents asked the legislature to construct a new county seat on the rail line, and Valdosta was created. The town is named for former governor George Troup's plantation, Val d'Aosta.

Smyrna   Located in southern Cobb County, Smyrna is a close suburb of Atlanta. The area was popular as the site of Smyrna Camp Ground, a religious encampment established in the late 1830s. The arrival of the Western and Atlantic Railroad in 1842 boosted development even more. The city was incorporated as Smyrna in 1872, after being known as Varner's Station, Ruff's Siding, Neal Dow, and Ruff's Station.

East Point   Located in southern Fulton County, East Point got its name because it is at the eastern end of the Atlanta & West Point Railroad. The western point, of course, is called West Point. East Point began in 1870 with a few families that settled near the railroad. Eventually, two gristmills and a government distillery were built. By 1880, the town added a sawmill, a steam gin, and a post office. It also was a popular summer resort.

Rome   Like its sister city in Italy, Rome is built on seven hills. It was founded in 1834 by a group of men who decided on the name by putting their written choices into a hat and drawing one out. Colonel Daniel R. Mitchell picked the name Rome because of the hills and the river. After the legislature declared Rome a city in 1835, the county seat was moved there from Livingston. The city soon became a prime cotton market because of its access to the Gulf Coast via steamboats on the Coosa River. Development increased even more with the arrival of the railroads and the removal of the Cherokees.

Alpharetta   Located about 25 miles north of Atlanta, the site of Alpharetta was a stopping point for travelers in the 1830s because of the natural springs in the area. In the early 1850s, trading posts were opened, tents were erected, and the community was christened New Prospect Camp Ground. In 1858, Alpharetta was incorporated as the county seat of Milton County. Milton became part of Fulton County in the 1930s.

Peachtree City   Considered one of the most successful planned communities in the country, Peachtree City was chartered in Fayette County in 1959. A unique feature of Peachtree City is residents' use of golf carts to navigate the 70 miles of paved trails around the town.

Hinesville   The county seat of Liberty County, Hinesville is home to Fort Stewart. Established in 1837 and named after State Senator Charlton Hines, the town thrived before the Civil War as a center of commerce for farms and plantations producing cotton, indigo, rice, and pine products such as turpentine. Hinesville and much of Liberty County were devastated by General William T. Sherman's March to the Sea in 1864. The town's recovery was steady but slow until the opening of Fort Stewart in the 1940s revitalized the economy.

Georgia's Capitals

Here's something you need to know if you're going to help your kids with their Georgia history homework. How many capitals has Georgia had?

The answer is five: Savannah, Augusta, Louisville, Milledgeville, and Atlanta. Now here's how that happened.

Savannah was the logical choice as the capital when the nation declared its independence in 1776. After all, Savannah was Georgia's oldest and largest city. But plans had to be changed when the British captured the city in 1778. Georgia legislators fled and regrouped in Augusta, more than 120 miles up the Savannah River.

After the redcoats captured Augusta, the state government became a moving target. It assembled at Heard's Fort in 1780 and probably held a meeting in Wilkes County at some point during the next year. In 1782, after the British left Savannah, Georgia officials headed back toward the coast, pausing to make New Ebenezer a temporary, unofficial seat of government until they were sure no British troops were left in Savannah.

Until 1785, Georgia lawmakers alternated meetings between Augusta and Savannah. In 1786, Augusta was once again the chosen site. But some of the new settlers wanted a more centrally located capital. Louisville in Jefferson County was picked, but Augusta continued to operate as the seat of government until 1796. A new capitol building was constructed in Louisville, and the government moved in.

Seven years later, the legislators voted to move the capital yet again, to Milledgeville on the Oconee River. The new capitol building was constructed and ready for occupancy in 1807. Milledgeville served as the capital for 60 years.

In 1877, a vote to determine which city would be the capital was held, and Atlanta was the popular choice. In 1879, the legislature made it official.

Old Capitol building in Milledgeville
GEORGIA DEPARTMENT OF ECONOMIC DEVELOPMENT

Eventually, you newcomers will be able to create your own lists of favorite natural wonders in the state. Until then, here are some suggestions from Charles Seabrook, a nature writer whose "Wild Georgia" column appears in the *Atlanta Journal-Constitution*.

1. Okefenokee Swamp: World-famous wetland.

2. Marshes of Glynn: These coastal salt marshes inspired poet Sidney Lanier to write his famous poem.

3. Cumberland Island National Seashore: Former president Jimmy Carter called it one of his favorite places on earth.

4. Ossabaw Island: An unspoiled barrier isle.

5. Cabretta Beach, Sapelo Island: One of the Atlantic coast's most beautiful undeveloped beaches.

6. Woody Pond, Harris Neck National Wildlife Refuge: Thousands of egrets, herons, and endangered wood storks form nesting colonies in this McIntosh County refuge each spring.

7. Ebenezer Creek: This national natural landmark in Effingham County harbors 1,000-year-old bald cypress trees.

8. Altamaha River: The lower Altamaha is called "Georgia's Amazon" for the lush, junglelike growth on its banks.

9. Broxton Rocks Ecological Preserve: This rugged sandstone outcrop in

Okefenokee Swamp
GEORGIA DEPARTMENT OF ECONOMIC DEVELOPMENT

Coffee County has been sculpted over the centuries into fissures and shallow ravines that are now havens for rare plants.

10. Ohoopee Dunes State Natural Area: Sometimes called "Georgia's Desert" because of its dry, sandy soil and scrubby vegetation, this section of Emanuel County is described by biologists as "an enchanting environment."

11. Wade Tract Preserve: This privately owned 200-acre swath of old-growth longleaf pines and wire grass in Thomas County is one of the few remaining examples of the great longleaf forest that once covered the Coastal Plain.

12. Providence Canyon State Park: This eroded land in Stewart County has been transformed into a place of great beauty. It's sometimes called Georgia's "Little Grand Canyon."

13. Doe Run Pitcher Plant Bog Natural Area: Lush growths of carnivorous pitcher plants emerge in spring in this part of Colquitt County.

14. Pine Mountain: President Franklin D. Roosevelt often came to this place in Harris County to enjoy the scenic views and to picnic and meditate.

15. Warm Springs: Roosevelt came to these bubbling springs in Meriwether County to treat his polio.

16. Oaky Woods Wildlife Management Area: See for yourself why conservationists are intent on saving from development this Houston County place of roaming black bears and rare wildflower habitats.

17. George L. Smith State Park: Bald cypresses growing in this Emanuel County park's pond are magnificent in the fall, when they take on orange-bronze tints.

18. Sprewell Bluff State Park: This little-known gem on the Flint River in Upson and Talbot counties has a three-mile trail that offers superb views of the river and rocky cliffs.

19. Palisades Unit, Chattahoochee River National Recreation Area: A spectacular green space in the midst of Metro Atlanta.

20. Graves Mountain: Rock hounds from all over the world come to Lincoln County for the amazing array of rocks and minerals.

21. Stone Mountain/Arabia-Davidson Mountain/Panola Mountain: These huge geological wonders sport some of Georgia's most colorful arrays of wildflowers in spring and fall.

22. Tallulah Gorge: Granite walls form steep cliffs at this Rabun County attraction.

23. Amicalola Falls State Park: The Dawson County falls plunge 729 feet in seven cascades to form the highest waterfall east of the Mississippi River.

24. Richard Russell Scenic Highway: Although it's not a natural wonder, this 14-mile road winds through some of the most splendid mountain scenery in the Southeast.

25. Cloudland Canyon State Park: One of Georgia's most scenic state parks, this Dade County attraction features rugged geology and beautiful vistas.

BOOKS AND RESOURCES

New Georgia Encyclopedia. www.georgiaencyclopedia.org.

Ray, Janisse. *Ecology of a Cracker Childhood.* Minneapolis, Minn.: Milkweed Editions, 1999.

Seabrook, Charles. *Cumberland Island: Strong Women, Wild Horses.* Winston-Salem, N.C.: John F. Blair, Publisher, 2004.

34 : *Newcomer's Guide to Georgia*

History

Etowah Indian Mounds State Historic Site in Cartersville
GEORGIA DEPARTMENT OF ECONOMIC DEVELOPMENT

Contrary to popular belief, the history of Georgia did not begin with the arrival of General James Oglethorpe and English settlers in 1733. Two hundred years before Oglethorpe, Hernando de Soto and other Spanish explorers established outposts in Georgia. They were soon followed by Jesuit and Franciscan missionaries.

Moreover, nearly 10,000 years before the Spanish came, the land that is now known as Georgia was home to prehistoric tribes that left few traces of their existence, other than some primitive stone tools and weapons. A large effigy of an eagle created with stones of different sizes and shapes is located in Putnam County. No one knows who built it, and for what purpose. Archaeologists have few clues to the fate of these early people.

The second stage in Georgia's history—the Mississippian period—lasted from about 800 A.D. to 1600 A.D. The people during this time were less nomadic and more agricultural. They lived in pole structures and created walls by weaving limbs and cane around the poles.

The Mississippian people also built large mounds that could have been used for religious activities, meetings, or burial grounds. One of the largest mound sites is at Etowah near Cartersville.

Many of the tribes were wiped out when Europeans came with smallpox and other diseases for which the Native Americans had no immunity. The ones who survived gathered to form the Creeks, Cherokees, and Seminoles. The Seminoles later moved into Florida, leaving the Creeks and the Cherokees to deal with the next influx of white settlers, led by Oglethorpe.

It's a common misconception, even among native Georgians, that Oglethorpe brought a bunch of convicts and debtors. In fact, the selection process was more intense than for other emigrants at the time. Oglethorpe wanted men and women of good character who had fallen on hard times. Only a small percentage had ever been in debtors' prison.

The first 35 families landed in Charleston, South Carolina, on January 13, 1733, after two months on rough seas. Oglethorpe, fearing the passengers would never return to the ship if allowed to go into Charleston, went ashore alone. The ship, the *Anne*, continued on to temporary barracks in Port Royal, and Oglethorpe located a site on the banks of the Savannah River as the place to begin his colony.

Fortunately for the newcomers, they met a friendly Creek chief, along with a trader, John Musgrove, and his daughter, Mary, who could interpret the Creek language. Following an exchange of gifts, the Indians agreed to give the settlers land on the Savannah for their town.

The settlement was saved from an epidemic caused by tainted drinking water from shallow wells when a shipload of Jewish families arrived with a doctor, Samuel Nunis. Nunis treated the sick and charged no fees. Once a deep well was dug in the middle of town to provide fresh water, the epidemic ended.

Soon, other immigrants began arriving from Europe. These included German Lutherans escaping religious persecution; Moravians, who moved on to Pennsylvania after refusing to bear arms against any enemies; and Scots, who had no problem at all with fighting.

As the settlement grew, so did the problems. When Oglethorpe returned in 1736 from his first trip back to London, he reaffirmed the rules that no rum would be sold and that Georgia would have no black slaves. But mounting debts led the settlers to sign a written protest allowing slavery, saying they could not survive as planters or traders in competition with South Carolina and other colonies that had slaves. The trustees modified the rules in 1749, allowing four slaves for every household that had at least one white male indentured servant. One year later, they abolished any restraints on slavery and land ownership.

Thereafter, Oglethorpe returned to his main duties as a soldier. Hostilities between England and Spain were heating up in the War of Jenkins' Ear. In 1742, Spain sent 50 ships toward St. Simons. In the skirmish known as the Battle of Bloody Marsh, Oglethorpe was successful in defeating the Spanish, driving them from Georgia, and restoring his reputation as a military leader. The colony's fate was secure for now.

Colonial Period

Once the Spanish threat was removed and slavery was allowed, Georgia began to flourish economically. Plantations along the marshy coast grew rice; indigo and other crops thrived inland; and timber was plentiful for logs, turpentine, and tar. Despite having all of these raw materials, Georgia still depended on other colonies and England for manufactured goods.

Georgia's first royal governor, naval captain John Reynolds, proved unpopular with the people. Under him, the assembly unwisely passed a terrible law that was soon repealed. The law provided a bounty to Indians for the scalp of any slave killed while running away. It also required a permit for any slave to leave his or her home plantation and banned slaves from traveling at night in groups of more than seven and from holding large assemblies. They could not be taught to read and write and were not allowed to own boats. Slaves also were forbidden to learn carpentry, masonry, and other skilled trades, but this law was ignored on most plantations.

While the French and Indian War was raging in the North, Reynolds's effort to recruit two regiments of Georgians failed for lack of interest. Georgians much preferred to trade with Indians than to fight them. Reynolds was recalled to England for overspending on forts along the Georgia coast.

His 1757 replacement, Henry Ellis, was a scientist with a diplomat's personality. He settled a claim by Mary Musgrove about ownership of St. Catherines Island and enlisted her help in making a treaty with the Cherokees. Illness forced Ellis to return to England in 1760.

Ellis's successor, James Wright, governed Georgia for 22 turbulent years. To celebrate the end of the French and Indian War in 1763, Wright, acting on the king's orders, invited 700 Creeks, Cherokees, Chickasaws, Choctaws, and Catawbas to Augusta for a meeting with the governors of North and South Carolina and Virginia. A treaty of friendship was signed, but more importantly, the Creeks ceded land to Georgia north beyond Augusta.

The Indian threat subsided, but a more serious one began to emerge: taxation without representation. The stamp tax of 1765 was enacted to help pay off England's debts from the French and Indian War. In Georgia, the stamp agent was burned in effigy. The legislature eventually relented, however, and Georgia became the only colony to use stamps. Outraged South Carolinians threaten to boycott Georgia businesses for what they considered an act of betrayal.

The Stamp Act was repealed in 1766, but the seeds of discontent had been sown. When a group of New England Puritans moved to Georgia to share in its prosperity, they brought with them Lyman Hall, a doctor, minister, and rice planter with a spirit of independence. He was Georgia's delegate to the Continental Congress and later became governor.

The 1767 Townshend Acts, which levied import duties on tea, glass, lead, and painters' colors, rekindled the dissent sparked by the Stamp Act. A group of patriot radicals including Noble W. Jones, Archibald Bulloch, John Houston, and George Walton began holding meetings and corresponding with patriots in other colonies. When news of the bloodshed at Lexington, Massachusetts, reached Georgia, a group of patriots stole 500 pounds of powder in Savannah, sent part to patriots in South Carolina, and hid the rest. The governor offered a reward of 150 pounds for the thieves, but no one stepped forward.

Georgia finally committed itself to the cause of independence at the Second Continental Congress. Meanwhile, Governor Wright's rule came to an end when a battalion of patriots formed under the leadership of Lachlan McIntosh, Samuel Elbert, and Joseph Habersham. Habersham, under orders to arrest Wright, marched into the governor's house and told Wright he was his prisoner. Wright was paroled with the promise he would not leave town. But a month later, he slipped past guards and boarded the British ship *Scarborough*.

On July 4, 1776, three Georgians—Button Gwinnett, Lyman Hall, and George Walton—signed their names to the Declaration of Independence. When word reached Savannah, a celebration erupted with cannon fire and the hanging of George III in effigy. Even before the celebratory shouts ended, Georgians began preparing for war.

The Revolutionary War

Refusing an offer of an olive branch from the king, the patriots thwarted a

British attempt to capture 11 ships loaded with Georgia rice that were bottled up in the Savannah River. In the wake of the hostilities, the provincial congress fled to Augusta and created a document setting up a new government in Georgia that provided for a president and a safety council. Archibald Bulloch was elected the first president. Button Gwinnett succeeded Bulloch upon his death a year later.

The Revolutionary War in Georgia was not simply between the colonists and the crown. Patriot families fought Tory families, and old feuds were settled that had nothing to do with the war. Gwinnett, who was commander in chief of the Georgia forces, decided he would lead an expedition against St. Augustine and succeed where others had failed. The poorly planned attack proved disastrous. As a result, Gwinnett was defeated in the next election by Lachlan McIntosh, who openly gloated about Gwinnett's defeat. Gwinnett subsequently challenged him to a duel. Both men were wounded, and Gwinnett died 12 days later. His death created a rift between the supporters of McIntosh and those of Gwinnett.

General Robert Howe, the new commander of the Southern division of the Continental Army, proved as poor a leader as Gwinnett. While defending the city of Savannah, Howe refused to listen to the advice of his officers, who suggested he should deploy his troops differently. One night, an old black man, Quamino Dolly, led British troops on a secret path through the swamps to the rear of Howe's forces. Howe was later court-martialed and acquitted.

The low point of the war for the patriots in Georgia came in 1780, when Lieutenant Colonel Elijah Clarke attacked the British in Augusta. Clarke was forced to withdraw, leaving his wounded men behind. Unfortunately, the Tory commander, Colonel Thomas Brown, still had bitter memories of being tarred and feathered by "the Liberty Boys." He ordered 13 wounded men to be brought into his house and hanged.

In 1781, Major General Nathanael Greene ordered Lieutenant Colonel Henry "Light Horse Harry" Lee to join Clarke in another attack on Augusta. Brown, the commander who had hanged Clarke's men, surrendered on June 5. Lord Cornwallis surrendered at Yorktown, Virginia, in October 1781. Except for some isolated skirmishes, the war was over.

The New State

Although the war with Great Britain was over, the newly free and independent Georgians faced problems. Veterans and loyalists had to be rewarded, the Creeks and Cherokees had to be dealt with as more settlers moved in, and a new government had to be organized.

Land grants, which had begun during the war for volunteers who would enlist for at least three years, continued. A new class system emerged as yeoman farmers were given land, as bankers, lawyers, and merchants acquired property, and as cotton plantation owners grew wealthier. At the bottom of the heap, just above the slaves, were the poor whites and tenant farmers.

With land available for four or five cents an acre, the system was ripe for speculation and corruption. In 1795, the state, after bribes were paid to legislators, sold nearly 50 million acres for a little more than a penny an acre to the Georgia Yazoo Company. When the scandal went public, riots broke out. The new legislature rescinded the Yazoo Act. But the law passed by the new legislature was later ruled unconstitutional by the United States Supreme Court, and the original Yazoo Act was ruled valid, no matter how corrupt. After that, Georgia used a lottery system for land sales.

One of the most significant events in Georgia history occurred in 1793 when Eli Whitney was visiting General Nathanael Greene's widow in Mulberry Grove near Savannah. At Mrs. Greene's suggestion, Whitney devised a machine for separating the short fibers of upland cotton from the seeds. Whitney's cotton gin changed the future of Georgia and the South, making it possible for more farmers to produce upland cotton where the long-staple sea-island cotton would not grow. The expansion of cotton growing, however, also meant the expansion of slavery. The number of slaves in Georgia increased from 60,000 in 1800 to more than 460,000 in 1860.

Another historic event occurred in 1827, when gold was discovered at Dahlonega in northeastern Georgia. The Cherokees who lived there didn't have a chance as more and more whites poured into the area. Then, in 1838, the United States Army began the relocation of 16,000 Cherokees to Oklahoma in a journey called the Trail of Tears. A small group of Cherokees fled into the mountains of North Carolina.

Georgia made much progress in the years before the Civil War. The state set aside land for the University of Georgia in Athens; the first newspaper, the *Augusta Chronicle and Gazette*, was published; and plans were made for the Medical Academy of Georgia. Steam locomotives took the place of riverboats. By the time the war broke out, Georgia was crisscrossed with railroads. The first textile mill and mill village in the South were built just across the river from Augusta.

The winds of secession blew strong in the 1850s as the issue of slavery divided the country. Georgia governor Joseph E. Brown argued that it was time to dissolve the Union, while Alexander H. Stephens urged everyone to wait and see what Abraham Lincoln would do if elected. His voice was drowned out by the secessionists. On January 19, 1861, Georgia followed South Carolina, Mississippi, Florida, and Alabama in leaving the Union.

The Civil War

As the war began, factories that had produced clothing and agricultural equipment switched to making uniforms and weapons; churches donated their iron bells; and thousands of young men flocked to join the Confederate army.

When Union blockades of Savannah and Charleston cut off shipping, Georgians were forced to scale back their cotton production to grow grain and vegetables to feed themselves and their livestock.

Until General William T. Sherman led his fiery march through the state, few battles were fought on Georgia soil. Federal gunboats were rebuffed in their attempt to take Fort McAllister but continued to raid plantations along the coast.

One of the more daring exploits in Georgia during the war is known as "the Great Locomotive Chase." This occurred in 1862 when Union captain James M. Andrews and 21 of his men dressed in civilian clothes boarded at Marietta with the intention of seizing the train and destroying the tracks. When the train stopped in Big Shanty (now Kennesaw), Andrews and his

Atlanta Cyclorama depicting the Battle of Atlanta in 1864
GEORGIA DEPARTMENT OF ECONOMIC DEVELOPMENT

men uncoupled the engine (known as "the General") and three freight cars and headed north. The conductor, the engineer, and a foreman pursued the locomotive on foot, later got on a flatcar, and finally acquired another engine (known as "the Texas") and ran it backward. When the General ran out of wood and steam near Ringgold, Andrews and his men were forced to flee into the woods. He and seven others were captured and later hanged as spies.

Georgia finally became a battleground in 1863 when Confederate general Braxton Bragg retreated from Chattanooga to engage in a two-day fight at a creek named Chickamauga—an Indian word meaning "river of death." By the end of the bloody battle, 18,000 Confederates and 16,000 Union soldiers were killed or wounded.

Sherman's March to the Sea began in 1864. Despite valiant opposition by General Joseph E. Johnston at encounters at Allatoona, New Hope Church, and Kennesaw, Sherman proceeded to burn Atlanta and destroy nearly everything in his path. After General Robert E. Lee's surrender at Appomattox, Georgia's Confederate leaders were briefly imprisoned and then paroled. President Jefferson Davis attempted to flee but was captured in Irwin County and sent to prison for two years at Fort Monroe.

Much of Georgia had been destroyed, but so had the institution of slavery. Now, the people faced another war—a political war of revenge.

Reconstruction

The assassination of Abraham Lincoln in 1865 destroyed any hopes Georgia and the South had of benevolent treatment after the rebellion. On the positive side, there were no mass executions of Confederate leaders. Only Henry Wirz, commander of the Andersonville prison, where thousands of Union prisoners died, was sentenced to hang. On the negative side, the Radical Republicans of the North were determined to get their revenge by political means. Dividing the South into five military districts, they formed governments giving blacks the right to vote and placed military commanders in charge of registration and voting.

Political maneuvering continued for years, first with black legislators being expelled from the legislature, then with white members of the state legislature and the United States Congress being unseated. The state went under military rule again before a final Reconstruction Act made it an act of rebellion to exclude anyone from office by reason of race or "previous condition of servitude."

Although more bitter days were ahead, Georgians were cheered somewhat by humorous and entertaining essays by newspapermen Bill Arp (the pen name for Charles H. Smith) and Joel Chandler Harris. Harris later became associate editor of the *Atlanta Constitution* and author of the Uncle Remus tales. Harris's nostalgic stories reminded Georgians of happier times before the war.

Republican rule ended in 1870 when Democrats took control of the Georgia House and Senate. Hated Republican governor Rufus Bullock secretly resigned and headed for Chicago.

The New South

After the war and Reconstruction, many in the South were reluctant to admit that the old way of life was literally gone with the wind. But a few leaders encouraged Georgians to look toward the future instead of yearning for the past. One of these was Henry Grady, the young editor of the *Atlanta Constitution*. At the New England Society in New York in 1885, Grady was scheduled to speak following an address by General Sherman, perhaps the most hated man in Georgia. Sherman, almost apologetic in his remarks about what he had done during the war, blamed politicians for inciting the hostilities.

In response, Grady said that the Old South of slavery and secession was dead, that there was a New South of union and freedom. He continued by unexpectedly praising Abraham Lincoln as "the first typical American, the first who comprehended within himself all the strength and gentleness, all the majesty and grace of this republic." He added his respects to Sherman with a touch of humor, describing him as an able man, but one some Georgians thought had been a little careless about fire. Grady concluded by promising that Atlanta had arisen as a "brave and beautiful city" from the ashes Sherman left and that "somehow or other we have caught the sunshine in the brick and mortar of our homes and have builded therein not one ignoble prejudice or memory."

Grady's New South speech was reported in the *New York Times* and praised throughout the North. It marked the end of one era and the beginning of a new, progressive one. In later speeches, Grady called for the South to free itself from dependence on cotton as its major crop and to diversify into other crops and new industry.

Grady and most white Georgians feared that only one thing could disrupt their march into the future: the black vote. As the Democratic Party once again took control in Georgia, laws were passed that effectively disenfranchised blacks. Literacy tests were required, and when those failed to keep blacks from the polls, fear tactics were used. The Ku Klux Klan, wearing their white robes and hoods, terrorized black families on the eve of elections and burned crosses in their yards at midnight. The threats and acts of violence ensured that no blacks would attempt to vote until the civil-rights movement of the next century.

Grady's dream of a New South would come true for merchants, industrialists, doctors, lawyers, and wealthy landowners, but poor farmers, both black and white, found themselves in a new kind of servitude. Those who could not afford land became sharecroppers or tenant farmers, providing labor in return for sharing the profits with the owners, who furnished the seed and fertilizer. Most of the time, sharecroppers broke even or ended the year in debt to the owners.

The economic picture was brighter in the cities, particularly Atlanta. In 1881, the World's Fair and Great International Cotton Exposition opened in Atlanta to show how much progress had been made. After the fair closed, the Exposition Cotton Mill moved into the main building and employed 500 workers. Because of its railroads, Atlanta became an important manufacturing and distribution center.

In 1886, druggist John S. Pemberton concocted a refreshing drink that would enrich many Atlantans and become famous around the world. He called it Coca-Cola.

The educational front saw progress as well. Schools that later would become the Georgia Institute of Technology, Agnes Scott College, and Berry College were founded. In Atlanta, doors opened for black students at Morehouse College, Clark University, Spelman College, and Morris Brown College.

Populism and Politics

Grady, who died unexpectedly in 1889, was an advocate of business and industry. The man who followed him as one of the most controversial and powerful political leaders in Georgia did not share Grady's vision. Tom Watson, born on a plantation in Columbia County in 1856, witnessed the loss of much of his family's land and wealth to creditors after the Civil War. Blaming an economic system that favored wealthy capitalists, Watson set out to become the voice of farmers and laborers, both black and white.

A fiery orator, Watson was elected to Congress in 1890 as a Democrat and quickly established a reputation as a rebel against his own party. The most important bill he sponsored was one creating rural free delivery of United States mail, a godsend to folks who lived in isolation on dirt roads.

Watson was a champion of the Alliance, an organization of farmers that supported crop diversification, regulation of railroads, a revised tax system, and the abolishment of the system of leasing convicts to private companies.

Eventually, the Alliance split into two factions—the small farmers, or "woolhat boys," and the "plughat crowd" from Atlanta, who had recently joined the Alliance. By 1892, a third political party, including members of the Georgia Alliance, formed as the Populists. Watson was the Populist choice for governor, a race he could have won easily. But he ran for Congress again and lost.

The economic panic of 1893 was disastrous nationally as well as in Georgia. The price of cotton hit its lowest mark in history; displaced tenant farmers wandered the roads looking for work and shelter; and mill workers who still had jobs were paid a mere thirty-six cents a day.

Watson, observing this economic collapse as editor of the *People's Party Paper*, reminded his readers that many of the reforms the Democrats were calling for were Populist Party positions he had advocated. Buoyed by the support of the Populists, Watson ran for Congress in 1894. He lost the initial election, but corruption at the polls resulted in a special runoff. This time, he won nine of the 11 counties but lost the election because the black vote in one ward in Augusta was 989 to nine against him. Angered at what he considered a betrayal by the blacks whose rights he had once supported, Watson added them to a list of his enemies that included Catholics and Jews.

After his defeat, Watson began publishing *Tom Watson's Magazine*, a publication supporting Populist views while bitterly attacking capitalists and advocating white supremacy. His support of Hoke Smith helped elect Smith as governor in 1906 on a platform that would raise taxes on railroads and legally eliminate blacks from politics.

Smith's election resulted in one of the worst race riots in Atlanta history. After rumors spread of several assaults on white women by blacks, mobs of angry whites attacked blacks in the streets. When the riot ended four days later, two whites and 10 blacks had been killed and more than 60 blacks had been wounded.

Watson continued to fan the flames of racial and religious hatred for the next decade. In 1913, Leo Frank, the Jewish manager of a pencil factory in Atlanta, was convicted of killing Mary Phagan, a 13-year-old employee. When the date of Frank's execution was delayed, Watson called for a lynching. After Governor John M. Slaton commuted Frank's death sentence, a mob of armed men took Frank out of prison and lynched him in Marietta.

The Frank case resulted in an outbreak of anti-Semitism. In 1915, the Ku Klux Klan was revived at a meeting and a fiery cross burning atop Stone Mountain. Watson reportedly was not present, but his vitriolic editorials were blamed for creating an atmosphere of hatred and bigotry in the state.

Watson was later elected to the United States Senate, where he opposed the League of Nations, Prohibition, and the American Legion and favored isolationism. When he died in 1922, more than 7,000 people attended his funeral.

The Boll Weevil and the Talmadge Era

The Georgia economy improved substantially after World War I. Cotton was profitable, but farmers also turned to other crops such as peanuts, corn, tobacco, and pecans. Pine forests were untapped resources for the emerging paper industry. Moonshiners who made illegal whiskey prospered during Prohibition.

Everything looked promising until the arrival of the boll weevil, a tiny insect that migrated from Mexico into the South and destroyed cotton crops by the millions. Georgia cotton farmers lost more than a third of their crops between 1915 and 1923. More than 60,000 farms failed. Families who had farmed for years headed north for jobs or moved into towns to work in textile mills.

While the state suffered with the rest of the country during the Great Depression, Governor Richard B. Russell was responsible for a reorganization of government that reduced more than 100 boards and bureaus to 18 and streamlined the university system with a board of regents. When Russell left office to become a United States senator, another politician came on the scene to resume the rhetoric of populism that Tom Watson had preached.

Eugene Talmadge dominated Georgia politics for years by arguing for the rights of the little man while quietly accepting contributions from big business. His two heroes were Napoleon and Tom Watson. Once he entered politics, Talmadge downplayed his background as a fraternity boy, Phi Beta Kappa graduate of the University of Georgia, and lawyer. He presented an image of

Georgia Governor Eugene Talmadge makes a speech on the campaign trail.
COURTESY OF GEORGIA ARCHIVES, VANISHING GEORGIA COLLECTION GEO 131-83

a tobacco-chewing, overall-wearing farm boy, often dressing the part with red suspenders. When he was elected governor, he put chicken coops in the backyard of the governor's mansion and briefly let cows graze on the lawn.

He was famous for fiery speeches delivered in a circuslike atmosphere. Fiddlin' John Carson would provide the music, and paid supporters planted in the crowd would cheer Talmadge on.

Talmadge always contended he was a friend of labor, but when textile unions tried to organize in Georgia, the mill owners who contributed to Talmadge's campaigns urged him to send in the state militia. Two strikers were killed and thousands arrested in the ensuing confrontations. After that, Talmadge could no longer count on the labor vote.

Talmadge was chosen governor four times but lost the election in 1942 to Ellis Arnall. Talmadge blamed his loss on a black widow spider bite he received at an outdoor privy that cut his campaigning short.

Arnall was responsible for reforming Georgia's penal system after the movie *I Am a Fugitive from a Chain Gang* created a flood of negative publicity. Arnall banned whippings and shackles and chains on convicts.

Georgia entered World War II with patriotic fervor. Some 320,000 Georgians served, and 6,754 were killed or missing in action. Since the draft age was 18, Arnall adopted the slogan, "Old enough to fight, old enough to vote," and lowered the voting age from 21 to 18.

Talmadge's last hurrah created a political incident known as "the Three Governors Controversy." In 1946, Talmadge was elected for the fourth time but died before he could be inaugurated. Legally, the lieutenant governor–elect, Melvin Thompson, should have been the next governor, but the general assembly decided it would elect Talmadge's successor. Eugene Talmadge's son, Herman Talmadge, received the most votes, but the incumbent governor, Ellis Arnall, refused to relinquish the office. Herman Talmadge forcibly took over the mansion and the office for 67 days, but neither he nor Arnall was able to do anything because Secretary of State Ben Fortson hid the Great Seal and refused to affix it to papers signed by either man. The Georgia Supreme Court finally resolved the issue by declaring Thompson governor.

Civil Rights and Changes

Like the rest of the country, Georgia enjoyed a boom in population and prosperity after World War II. But another battle loomed, one that would divide blacks and whites for the next two decades and beyond. In 1948, President Harry Truman proposed a civil-rights program that would outlaw lynching. For years, Georgia and Mississippi had the unfortunate distinction of being known as the lynching capitals of the world. Truman's proposal also would eliminate separate seating for whites and blacks on interstate trains and buses and would require equal treatment in employment.

Georgia attempted to forestall integration by setting up "separate but equal" schools for blacks and whites. In most cases, the schools were separate but definitely not equal. In 1954, the United States Supreme Court ruled that segregation should be ended "with all deliberate speed." In Georgia and other Southern states, "deliberate speed" meant years of delay. *Atlanta Constitution* editor Ralph McGill was one of the moderates who opposed the activities of the Ku Klux Klan and appealed for racial fairness.

Integration still came slowly to Georgia. Pools and playgrounds in Atlanta were closed to blacks. Blacks who attempted to sit in the front of Atlanta city buses were arrested. The first black students—Charlayne Hunter and Hamilton Holmes—were admitted to the University of Georgia in 1961, and black students were admitted to Atlanta public schools later that year.

The violence over integration that occurred in Alabama and some other states was largely avoided in Georgia because of the actions of Governor Carl Sanders and Atlanta mayor Ivan Allen, Jr. As new businesses moved into

The Rev. Martin Luther King Jr. presents a copy of his first book, Strength to Love, *to Eula Branham, a teacher at North Avenue Elementary School, at Ebenezer Church in 1963.*
Courtesy of Georgia Archives, Vanishing Georgia Collection geo 063-92

Atlanta, Allen proclaimed it "a city too busy to hate."

Old fears died hard, however. In 1966, Lester Maddox surprised the pundits by defeating Ellis Arnall for governor. Maddox was a staunch segregationist who became a folk hero to some Georgians when he and his son brandished an ax handle as blacks attempted to enter the family's fried-chicken restaurant. Lester Maddox later closed the restaurant rather than integrate it.

Georgia survived Maddox's tenure and gradually came to accept integration as the law of the land, due to the efforts of the Reverend Martin Luther King, Jr., Andrew Young, Ralph David Abernathy, and other civil-rights leaders of the Southern Christian Leadership Conference. It also helped that Jimmy Carter was elected as a moderate and progressive governor in 1970. In 1976, Carter stunned political experts by defeating incumbent Gerald Ford in the presidential race.

Although racial prejudice has not been stamped out, changes since the turbulent 1960s have been dramatic. In 1973, Maynard Jackson of Atlanta was the first African-American elected mayor of a Southern city. Jackson was serving his third term as mayor when Atlanta was selected as the host city for the 1996 Olympics. The Olympics, along with the rapid growth of businesses and the influx of Asian and Hispanic immigrants, made Atlanta an international city.

After two terms, Jackson was succeeded as Atlanta mayor by Andrew Young, who also served as a United States congressman and United Nations ambassador. In 2002, Shirley Franklin of Atlanta became the first black woman elected mayor of a major Southern city.

State politics saw a power shift as Republicans gained control of the legislature and George "Sonny" Perdue defeated Democratic incumbent Roy Barnes in 2002 to become the state's first Republican governor since Reconstruction.

Other changes have taken place as the population of Georgia has grown and become more diverse. Suburbanites and empty nesters are selling their houses, flocking to the cities, and moving into condominiums and lofts. Small towns that once were practically abandoned are thriving thanks to architectural facelifts and new restaurants, shops, parks, and in-town residences. The New South that Henry Grady envisioned in 1885 is now a reality.

Historic Sites

Native American Sites

Chieftains Museum: 800 Riverside Parkway, Rome, Ga. 30162 (706-291-9494). Built in 1794, this log cabin home of Cherokee leader Major Ridge is now a museum with artifacts detailing the story of the Cherokees and their removal to Oklahoma. See photograph on next page.

Etowah Indian Mounds: 813 Indian Mounds Road, Cartersville, Ga. 30120 (770-387-3747). These mounds—some at least 60 feet tall—offer a glimpse into what life was like for Native Americans from 900 A.D. to 1500 A.D. The mounds were used as places of worship or burial sites for tribal leaders.

New Echota: 1211 Chatsworth Highway, Calhoun, Ga. 30701 (706-624-1321). Once the capital of the Cherokee Nation, the site now consists of a museum and a few restored buildings. One of the exhibits is the printing shop where the *Cherokee Phoenix*, a Native American newspaper, was printed in English and Cherokee.

Colonial Period

Battle of Bloody Marsh: Demere Road, St. Simons Island, Ga. 31522 (800-933-2627). This is the place where British troops defeated the Spanish on July 7, 1742, and prevented an attack on Fort Frederica.

Fort Frederica National Monument: 6515 Frederica Road, St. Simons Island, Ga. 31522 (912-638-3639). General James Oglethorpe built this fort in 1736 as a defense against the Spanish.

Chieftains Museum
GEORGIA DEPARTMENT OF ECONOMIC DEVELOPMENT

Revolutionary War

Fort Morris Historic Site: 189 Charlie Butler Road, Midway, Ga. 31320 (912-638-7472). The British captured this fort on January 9, 1779. After the Revolutionary War, the Americans renamed it Fort Defiance and used it against the British in 1812. Visitors can watch a film at the site's museum.

Kettle Creek Revolutionary War Battlefield: Ga. 44 (Warhill Road), Washington, Ga. 30673 (706-678-2013). The patriots defeated the British here on February 14, 1779, in the Continental Army's only major victory in Georgia.

Civil War

Andersonville National Historic Site: 496 Cemetery Road, Andersonville, Ga. 31711 (229-924-2558). Andersonville National Cemetery adjoins the National Prisoner of War Museum and the site of the stockade where more than 40,000 Union prisoners of war were held in intolerable conditions. Prison commandant Henry Wirz was convicted of war crimes and hanged. See photograph on page 52.

Atlanta Cyclorama: 800-C Cherokee Avenue, Atlanta, Ga. 30315 (404-624-1071). The world's largest panoramic painting depicts the Battle of Atlanta as it occurred on July 22, 1864. The narration is accompanied by music and sound effects. See photograph on page 41.

Chickamauga and Chattanooga National Military Park: 3370 Lafayette Road, Fort Oglethorpe, Ga. 30742 (706-866-9241). Commemorative

Andersonville National Historic Site

monuments for both the Blue and the Gray mark the site of one of the bloodiest battles of the war. A driving tour and video are available.

Confederate Cemetery/Battle of Resaca: U.S. 41 and Confederate Road, Resaca, Ga. 30735 (800-887-3811). Visitors can take a self-guided tour of this battlefield, the site of the first major battle in the Atlanta Campaign.

Fort McAllister Historic Park: 3894 Fort McAllister Road, Richmond Hill, Ga. 31324 (800-864-7275). The site where General Sherman ended his March to the Sea offers camping, boating, and a museum. Guests can visit original battery positions on the Ogeechee River.

Fort Pulaski National Monument: U.S. 80 East, Savannah, Ga. (912-786-5787). Built in the 1830s to defend Savannah, the fort was captured by Union forces early in the Civil War. It is open daily.

Kennesaw Mountain National Battlefield Park: 900 Kennesaw Mountain Drive, Kennesaw, Ga. 30152 (770-427-4686). The site of heavy fighting during the Atlanta Campaign in 1864, the park contains 3,000 acres of woodlands and trails. The welcome center is open daily.

Pickett's Mill Battlefield Historic Site: 4432 Mount Tabor Church Road, Dallas, Ga. 30157 (770-443-7850). This is one of the best-preserved Civil War battlefield sites in the country. The earthworks look much as they did when Confederate troops defeated Union troops on May 27, 1864, and delayed General Sherman's march for a week. A film is available at the site's museum, and visitors can follow trails used by the troops.

Port Columbus National Civil War Naval Museum: 1002 Victory Drive, Columbus, Ga. 31901 (706-327-9798). The museum displays the wooden hulls of two Confederate gunboats, the CSS *Jackson* and the CSS *Chattahoochee*, as well as replicas of the USS *Monitor* and the USS *Hartford*.

Other Sites

Andalusia Farm: U.S. 41 North, Milledgeville, Ga. 31061 (478-454-4029). The home of author Flannery O'Connor is open for tours.

Atlanta History Center: 130 West Paces Ferry Road, Atlanta, Ga. 30305 (404-814-4000). This museum features a large collection of Civil War artifacts and permanent and changing exhibits of Southern culture. Also on the grounds is the 1845 Tullie Smith Farm, surrounded by 33 acres of gardens.

Margaret Mitchell House and Museum: 990 Peachtree Street, Atlanta, Ga. 30309 (404-249-7015). The house where Margaret Mitchell wrote *Gone With the Wind* is open for tours. Photographs and writings from the author's early life are on display.

Martin Luther King Jr. National Historic Site: 450 Auburn Avenue, Atlanta, Ga. 30312 (404-331-6922). The civil-rights leader's birth home and Ebenezer Baptist Church, where he served as pastor, are open for daily tours.

Savannah History Museum: 303 Martin Luther King Jr. Boulevard, Savannah, Ga. 31401 (912-238-1779). Visitors can watch a film about the city's history from its beginnings in 1733 and enjoy exhibits about the Battle of Savannah during the Revolutionary War. Items of interest include dugout canoes from the 1800s, weapons and military uniforms, and the park bench used in the movie *Forrest Gump.*

Wren's Nest House Museum: 1050 Ralph David Abernathy Boulevard, Atlanta, Ga. 30310 (404-753-7735). The home of Joel Chandler Harris, author of the Uncle Remus tales, is now a museum that features storytelling hours.

Wren's Nest House Museum
GEORGIA DEPARTMENT OF ECONOMIC DEVELOPMENT

BOOKS AND RESOURCES

Cobb, James C. *Georgia Odyssey*. Athens: University of Georgia Press, 2008.

Coleman, Kenneth. *A History of Georgia*. Athens: University of Georgia Press, 1991.

Greene, Melissa Fay. *Praying for Sheetrock*. Addison-Wesley, 1991.

Lewis, John, with Michael D'Orso. *Walking With the Wind: A Memoir of the Movement*. New York: Simon & Schuster, 1998.

New Georgia Encyclopedia. www.georgiaencyclopedia.org.

Pomeranz, Gary M. *Where Peachtree Meets Sweet Auburn: The Saga of Two Families and the Making of Atlanta*. New York: Scribner's, 1996.

Roberts, Gene, and Hank Klibanoff. *The Race Beat: The Press, the Civil Rights Struggle and the Awakening of a Nation*. New York: Knopf, 2006.

Sullivan, Buddy, and the Georgia Historical Society. *Georgia: A State History*. Arcadia Publishing, 2003.

Tuck, Stephen G. N. *Beyond Atlanta: The Struggle for Racial Equality in Georgia, 1940-1980*. Athens: University of Georgia Press, 2001.

The State Government

Governor's Mansion
GEORGIA DEPARTMENT OF ECONOMIC DEVELOPMENT

You may not be interested in the structure of Georgia's government, but sooner or later you'll have to deal with one or more departments. And whether you like it or not, the government and the laws passed by the legislature affect everyone's life. So here's the basic information you need to know.

The Georgia Constitution is the framework of state government. Only the United States Constitution is a higher authority. The last revision of the Georgia Constitution was in 1983. Any amendment must be approved by two-thirds of the State House of Representatives and the State Senate and by a majority of the voters in the next general election.

Governor: The governor, the chief official of the executive branch, is elected to a four-year term. Only two successive four-year terms are allowed. The governor can make appointments to state agencies, propose laws and budgets for the legislature to consider, and veto laws that are passed.

Lieutenant governor: The lieutenant governor presides over the State Senate and carries out any other duties assigned by the governor.

Attorney general: Duties of the attorney general include acting as legal adviser for state agencies, state departments, and the governor; representing the state in capital felony appeals before the Supreme Court of Georgia; representing the state in all civil cases before the court; and conducting special investigations into questionable activity concerning stage agencies, state departments, and persons or companies that have done business with the state of Georgia.

Department of Agriculture: Established in 1874, this department has the missions of protecting and promoting agriculture and consumer interests and ensuring that agricultural products are safe. The department also publishes the *Farmers and Consumers Market Bulletin*, which is available by mail and online.

Department of Labor: This department is responsible for unemployment insurance, employment services, and vocational rehabilitation programs. It also oversees child labor issues and inspects amusement park and carnival rides, boilers, and pressure vessels.

Office of Insurance and Safety Fire Commissioner: This office is responsible for handling consumer questions and complaints about insurance. The state fire marshal handles building inspections, manufactured housing inspections, hazardous materials inspections, and licensing.

Public Service Commission: This commission votes on requests for rate hikes by electric, natural gas, telecommunications, and transportation companies and regulates these companies to ensure that consumers are getting reliable and reasonably priced services.

Secretary of State: This office handles professional licensing, voter registration, and balloting and is responsible for the Georgia State Archives, which preserves valuable historical documents and photographs.

State School Superintendent: The superintendent and the Georgia Department of Education oversee public education and are responsible for ensuring that state and federal funds to schools are properly allocated.

Legislative Branch

The Georgia General Assembly was formed in 1777 as a single house but became the House of Representatives and the Senate in 1789. All appropriations bills originate in the House and must be approved by both the House and the Senate before being sent to the governor. The Senate also must approve the governor's appointments.

The House has 180 members, while the Senate has 56. All are elected to two-year terms. The speaker of the House presides over that body and is elected every two years by the members. The lieutenant governor is the presiding officer of the Senate.

Both the Senate and the House are made up of committees that consider legislation and report on it before it can be considered by all the members on the chamber floor.

The Georgia General Assembly meets annually beginning the second Monday in January and ending in mid-March. One of the most important functions of the legislature is to enact a budget that sets funding for all state programs.

Judicial Branch

Judges in Georgia's judicial system are popularly elected by the state's voters. The system consists of courts of limited, general, and appellate jurisdiction.

Courts of limited jurisdiction include magistrate courts, which try violations of county ordinances and civil cases of less than $15,000. Probate courts administer estates. State courts hear civil cases and misdemeanor criminal cases. Juvenile courts consider cases involving youths under 17. Each county has its own magistrate, probate court, and juvenile court. Approximately 60 counties have a state court. Magistrate, probate, and juvenile judges decide cases without a jury, but state courts can provide a jury trial. Decisions of magistrates and probate judges can be appealed to superior court. Decisions of juvenile and state courts are appealed to appellate courts.

Criminal cases, civil cases, and all felonies are tried in superior court. Georgia has 48 superior court circuits, each circuit encompassing up to eight counties. Superior court must meet at least twice a year in each county in the circuit.

The two main courts of appellate jurisdiction are the court of appeals and the Georgia Supreme Court. The court of appeals has 12 judges and can consider any appeal from a trial court. The Georgia Supreme Court consists of seven justices who can hear any appeal involving the constitutionality of any law, as well as any cases requested by the court of appeals.

Counties

Georgia's 159 counties are the second-highest number of any state in the country (Texas has 254). The state's four consolidated city-counties are Athens (Clarke County), Augusta (Richmond County), Columbus (Muscogee County), and Cusseta (Chattahoochee County). Counties historically were created with the idea that a farmer should be able to get to the county seat and back in one day by wagon or on horseback. Additional counties were created after automobiles became common, and still others were created for political reasons.

Each county's government—usually a board of commissioners—is allowed under the Georgia Constitution to deal with any local matters, such as zoning and schools.

United States Congress

Georgia is represented by two senators and 13 members of Congress. Senators are elected every six years and congressmen every two years. For a list of elected officials, visit www.sos.georgia.gov.

Voting

Georgians are eligible to vote in any election if they are at least 18 years old, United States citizens, and legal residents of Georgia and the county in which they're voting. If you're not registered to vote, you can do so at your county's voter registration office, by motor voter registration, by mail-in application, or online at www.sos.georgia.gov.

One of the following forms of photo ID is required: a driver's license, even if expired; a valid state- or federal-government-issued ID, including free voter IDs issued by county registrars and the Georgia Department of Driver Services; a valid United States passport; a valid employee ID issued by a branch, department, or agency of the United States government, Georgia, or a county or municipality; a valid United States military ID; or a valid tribal ID.

Georgia's official fruit is the peach.
GEORGIA DEPARTMENT OF ECONOMIC DEVELOPMENT

Official Symbols

No, you do not have to pass a quiz on the state's symbols to qualify as a resident, but knowing that the green tree frog is the official amphibian and that the brown thrasher is the state bird will impress native Georgians. You'll impress them even more if you can recite the Georgian's Creed:

Accepting, as I do, the principles upon which Georgia was founded, not for self but others;—its Democratic form of Government, based on "Wisdom, Justice and Moderation";—its natural resources;—its Educational, Social and Religious advantages, making it a most desirable place to live—I will strive to be a pure upright Citizen, rejecting the evils—loving and emulating the good.

I further believe it is my duty to defend it against all enemies, to honor and obey its laws, to apply the Golden Rule in all my dealings with my fellow Citizens.

I feel a sense of pride in the history and heroic deeds accomplished by my forebears, and shall endeavor to so live that my State will be proud of me for doing my bit to make my State a better Commonwealth for future generations.

If you don't want to go that far, you can at least impress your fifth-grade son or daughter by knowing the following—

"Official" State Symbols, Facts, and Events

Art museum	Georgia Museum of Art
Ballet	Atlanta Ballet
Beef cookoff	"Shoot the Bull" barbecue at the Hawkinsville Civitan Club
Butterfly	Swallowtail
Crop	Peanut
Fish	Largemouth bass
Flower	Cherokee rose
Folk dance	Square dance
Folklife play	*Swamp Gravy*
Fossil	Shark tooth
Fruit	Peach
Game bird	Bobwhite quail
Gem	Quartz
Historic drama	*The Reach of Song*
Insect	Honeybee
Marine mammal	Right whale
Mineral	Staurolite
Motto	"Wisdom, justice and moderation"
Musical theater	Jekyll Island Musical Theatre Festival
Poet laureate	David Bottoms
Pork cookoff	Slosheye Trail Big Pig Jig
Possum	Pogo
Prepared food	Grits
Reptile	Gopher tortoise
Seashell	Knobbed whelk
Song	"Georgia on My Mind"
Tartan	Georgia tartan
Theater	Springer Opera House
Tree	Live oak
Vegetable	Vidalia sweet onion
Waltz	"Our Georgia"
Wildflower	Azalea

The new official state flag was created on May 8, 2003, the third in a period of 27 months, after a flag flap that probably influenced a gubernatorial election. Critics of the earlier flags protested the use of the Confederate battle flag as part of Georgia's state flag. The current flag, based on the first national flag of the Confederacy, consists of three horizontal bars of equal width—two red bars separated by a white bar. A square blue canton is in the upper left corner. A circle of 13 white stars in the center symbolizes Georgia and the 12 other original colonies. Georgia's coat of arms is within the circle of stars above the words "In God We Trust," both in gold.

RESOURCES

More information about the state government is available by visiting www.georgia.gov or the New Georgia Encyclopedia at www.georgiaencyclopedia.org.

The Economy

Cotton field
GEORGIA DEPARTMENT OF ECONOMIC DEVELOPMENT

Georgia's economy was based on agriculture in its early days. To a large extent, it still is. Now, it's not known simply as farming, but as agribusiness. Much of the state's economy today is based on farm and forest products. But the economy has diversified, just as the population has changed. The state is now home to high-tech industries; electronics, automobile, and textile manufacturing plants; retail stores; financial and educational institutions; and transportation facilities. Delta Airlines is based at Hartsfield-Jackson Atlanta International Airport. And countless millions of people around the world drink one of the many beverages produced by Atlanta's Coca-Cola Company.

Consider these statistics:

Forty-one of the largest 1,000 companies listed in *Fortune* magazine have headquarters in Georgia, including Coke, Delta, CNN/Turner Broadcasting, Equifax, The Home Depot, Aflac,

Savannah

Internet Security Systems, Ciba Vision, Intercontinental Hotels and Resorts, Earthlink, and UPS.

The state leads the world in the production of carpet, kaolin, chickens, and watermelons. Georgia is the 11th-largest exporting state in the country.

Savannah is the second-largest port in the Southeast.

Eighty percent of United States markets and consumers can be reached in two hours by air or in two days by truck from Georgia.

Hartsfield-Jackson Atlanta International Airport is one of the world's busiest airports, offering more than 500 direct flights to American and international cities.

Change in general has been good for the state, but Georgia has not been immune from national and global economic problems. The decline in sales for the American auto industry has resulted in cutbacks and projected closings of Ford and General Motors plants in the Atlanta area. Delta, one of the major airlines in the country, only recently emerged from bankruptcy and the elimination of several thousand jobs.

To better understand Georgia's economy today, let's take a look at how everything began and evolved.

Early Days

When the first colonists arrived in Georgia with General James Oglethorpe, their mission was to establish homes in the New World and repay England by sending back furs, skins, precious metals, silk, corn, indigo, rice, and cotton. They practiced farming not only to survive but to satisfy the mother country's need for commerce.

Oglethorpe was wise enough to ask Native Americans about their agricultural methods. Silk production also proved a success for the colonists, who shipped almost a ton of silk annually in the late 1760s. Since silk was much in demand among the aristocracy of Europe, England pressured the colonies to expand the industry. Oglethorpe established the Trustee Garden in Savannah for agricultural experiments and planted a number of mulberry trees, since silkworms feed on mulberry leaves.

Silk makers from Italy were brought to Georgia to teach the settlers how to process silk. The Salzburgers from Germany set up silk operations north of Savannah and succeeded for a while. Silkworms were susceptible to temperature changes, however, and the colonists turned to the more dependable crops of tobacco and cotton.

King Cotton

The early cotton grown was the sea-island variety, which had long fibers that were easily separated from the seeds. Sea-island cotton could be grown

Cotton harvesting
GEORGIA DEPARTMENT OF
ECONOMIC DEVELOPMENT

only along the coast because of the longer growing season. Upland cotton had shorter fibers and was much more difficult to remove from the seeds.

Cotton truly became king after Eli Whitney's cotton gin mechanized the separation of cotton fibers from seeds and allowed short-staple cotton to be planted profitably in other areas of Georgia. As cotton production expanded throughout the state, so did the importation of slaves to plant, hoe, and harvest the crop. By the beginning of the Civil War, some 68,000 farms in Georgia were growing cotton.

After the war, farmers began to realize that repeated plantings of cotton in the same fields depleted the soil. While some abandoned worn-out land and moved to more fertile farmland, others turned to diversification of crops and gradually improved the soil's fertility.

The arrival of the boll weevil in 1915 decimated cotton crops in Georgia and throughout the South, forcing many farmers to reduce their cotton plantings in favor of vegetables, poultry, and livestock. Others planted pine trees on acreage no longer suitable for cotton.

By the end of the 20th century, cotton farming had become mostly a corporate agribusiness involving mechanization, computerization, and planting on large tracts of land.

Today, cotton is still a significant money crop in Georgia. More than 1.5 million bales are harvested most years.

Textiles

During the mid-1800s, Georgia became a leader in turning its cotton into thread and cloth. Attempts to operate factories in the early 1800s had failed in Wilkes County, Jefferson County, and Morgan County primarily because the frontier market was not lucrative enough.

The "Nullification Crisis" during the 1820s was a sectional dispute over states' rights to nullify the tariff of 1828, which promoted American manufacturing over British competition. President Andrew Jackson was expected to reduce the tariff, and when he failed to do so, South Carolina declared the tariff unconstitutional. In 1833, the Force Bill was passed allowing Jackson to use military force against South Carolina. Fortunately, a new, lower tariff bill satisfactory to South Carolina also passed. The tariff policy would continue to be a divisive issue between the North and the South, one that would join slavery as a reason for the Civil War.

During the battle against tariffs, Georgia businessmen stepped up their

Textile mill at Columbus
GEORGIA DEPARTMENT OF ECONOMIC DEVELOPMENT

efforts at textile production. Augustin Clayton of Athens and William Schley of Augusta built cotton mills near their towns and soon boasted huge profits. By 1840, the state had 14 cotton mills with more than 16,000 spindles.

Impressed with the profitability of the textile industry, Georgia legislators passed laws in 1847 making incorporation easier for textile companies than for other companies. By 1849, the number of textile mills more than doubled, from 14 to 35. The textile boom was under way.

The mill owners began to employ new technology as they expanded. Mills were built at the falls on rivers and creeks to harness power for the machines. Other factories were steam powered. The coarse fabrics first produced in the mills were called "Georgia wool." Later, the mills made a heavier fabric called "cotton duck."

As the factories expanded, finding white workers became a problem. Some slaves were used, and experienced workers from Northern mills were encouraged to move to Georgia.

Shortly before the Civil War, the textile bubble burst because of overproduction, overexpansion, and competition from Northern factories. By 1860, some 33 textile factories survived in Georgia. The entrepreneurs who had placed their bets on textiles turned to other businesses, such as financial and insurance companies and papermaking. Some set up plants to manufacture the machinery for textile mills.

Factory owners and farmers had learned a valuable lesson from the three-decade economic roller-coaster ride. When farm profits increased, textile mill profits decreased, and vice versa. Wise investors after that never put all their money—or cotton bolls—in one basket.

The mills that remained open during the Civil War made uniforms and supplies for the Confederate army. Since most able-bodied men were fighting in uniform, the work force was made up mostly of women. Their success led Union general William T. Sherman to target the mills as a way of crippling the Confederate economy and hastening the end of the war. During his March to the Sea, he ordered his troops to round up the women workers at New Manchester Mill and Roswell Mill and deport them to the North so they could not work elsewhere in the Confederacy. Then he burned the mills.

Despite the abolition of slavery and the destruction of many plantations, cotton production bounced back after the war to become the most important part of the state's economy. But financial problems arising from the economic panic of 1873 resulted in a shift from an agricultural economy to an industrial one.

Henry W. Grady, a young editor at the *Atlanta Constitution*, was one of the voices calling for a New South to rise out of the ashes of the Old South. One of his solutions was to urge every Georgia town to build a cotton mill. New mills were constructed in the 1880s, and those abandoned or damaged during the war were rebuilt.

William Young rebuilt his Eagle Factory in Columbus and renamed it the Eagle and Phenix Mills. And in West Point, Civil War veterans Lafayette and Ward Lanier established West Point Manufacturing. Optimism returned to Georgians as Grady's bold vision of the economic future took shape.

As the textile industry prospered, Northern investors began looking to Georgia as a promised land of lower taxes, cheap labor, and no unions. More mills were built in Augusta, Columbus, Macon, and LaGrange. By the end of the 19th century, the Georgia School of Technology opened its Textile Department to train future managers and engineers for the state's 98 mills.

Georgia mill owners soon developed a system of mill villages that had been successful for New England factory owners. Begun in 1810 by New England mill owner Samuel Slater, the system involved providing company-owned housing for workers. This served two purposes: easy access for the workers and the creation of a sense of loyalty to the company among families living in the houses. The owners collected rent from the workers, the figure determined by how many family members worked in the mill.

Mill villages were a godsend to many families who moved from ramshackle farmhouses with no running water to decent housing. Sometimes, entire families, including wives and children, worked in the mills on different shifts. Two of the most famous mill villages in Georgia were Whitehall in Athens and

Cabbagetown in Atlanta. Many of the workers for the Fulton Bag and Cotton Mills migrated to Atlanta from Appalachia.

The textile industry prospered into the 20th century as mills such as Bibb Manufacturing of Macon began producing hosiery, carpet yarn, and other products. In Dalton, chenille bedspreads, traditionally made by hand and sold at roadside stands, were the inspiration for tufted textiles and the carpet industry. North Georgia became the carpet center of the world, producing 80 percent of the carpet products sold on the international market.

The textile industry faced some grim years after World War I. Families had lost members in the war and the influenza epidemic of 1918. Farmers had lost entire cotton crops to the boll weevil. New and more efficient machinery meant fewer workers were needed. The workers who kept their jobs were required to operate more machinery to increase production.

The mills provided welcome employment for both white and black workers, but the African-Americans usually ended up with the lowest-paying jobs. Even as late as the 1950s and early 1960s, blacks were not allowed to live in the mill villages.

Just after World War I, hundreds of thousands of African-Americans in Georgia and the rest of the South began what is known as "the Great Migration" to Chicago, Detroit, and other Northern cities where higher-paying jobs were available in mills and automobile factories.

More changes came during the Great Depression. Some mills shut down, and those that remained open were required to follow new rules under President Franklin D. Roosevelt's National Industry Recovery Act. Workers had to be at least 16, and the length of workdays was regulated. When mill owners refused to follow these rules, workers began to organize unions.

The clash between workers and management reached a crisis in the General Textile Strike of 1934, the largest labor protest in the history of the South. More than 170,000 Southern workers (along with 200,000 Northern workers) participated, including nearly 44,000 protesters in Georgia. Numerous incidents of violence took place in Georgia, and fatalities occurred in other states.

Governor Eugene Talmadge declared martial law and sent Georgia National Guardsmen to transport strikers from cotton mills in Coweta County to cells at Fort McPherson that had once held German prisoners of war. They were released when the strike ended three weeks later.

Anyone who thought the strikers had won was wrong. When they returned to their jobs, they found that working conditions had not improved. Those who had protested the loudest were evicted from their homes in the mill villages. It would take another world war before things changed for the better.

The World War II years were good ones for the textile industry in Georgia, as the mills landed government contracts for uniforms, gas masks, camouflage nets, and materials for parachutes. Jobs were plentiful for women and for men not eligible for the draft.

This period of prosperity extended through the 1950s, at least for the owners. As mills became more automated, workers were laid off and houses in the mill villages were sold.

More dramatic changes occurred upon the establishment of the Occupational Safety and Health Administration (OSHA). Owners who could not afford to update old and hazardous machinery simply shut down their mills. Others began outsourcing production to Asian markets where labor was cheap. By the mid-1990s, the number of textile workers was reduced to half of what it had been in the 1950s.

Textile manufacturing is still considered viable in Georgia because of the carpet industry and the availability of Hispanic workers. Meanwhile, many of the mills that have closed are being converted into other facilities. In Atlanta, for example, the Fulton Cotton Mill has been remodeled and rented as loft apartments.

Agribusiness

An estimated one in six Georgians works in agriculture, forestry, or a related field. More than 11 million acres of land in the state are devoted to farms. Georgia leads the nation in the production of peanuts, pecans, poultry, eggs, and rye. It is second in the country in cotton production and is one of the largest producers of peaches, watermelons, and tomatoes. The state's official onion, the Vidalia, is famous worldwide. Wheat, tobacco, soybeans, cottonseed, turf grass, and corn are also cultivated. Georgia is fifth in the country in tobacco acreage and first in the production of broilers, or young chickens.

The world's largest poultry company was formed when Pilgrim's Pride Corporation merged with Atlanta-based Gold Kist in 2006. Gold Kist was founded during the Great Depression by D. W. Brooks, an agronomy professor at the University of Georgia. Organized as the Cotton Producers Association (CPA), Brooks's cooperative helped farmers in Georgia market their cotton. CPA soon diversified to sell farm supplies and fertilizer. It became Gold Kist in 1974 and began to focus on poultry.

Vidalia onions
GEORGIA DEPARTMENT OF ECONOMIC DEVELOPMENT

Gold Kist provides farmers with chicken houses, labor, feed, equipment, and chicks. In return, the farmers sign contracts to raise the chickens. Gold Kist processes the mature birds and markets them. The deal allows farmers to reach global markets and reduces the risk of market fluctuations.

Cagle's, which began as a small family-owned shop in Atlanta in 1945, is another major poultry producer in Georgia, boasting $300 million in revenue. Cagle's chickens can be found in supermarkets and upscale restaurants and as chicken nuggets in fast-food restaurants.

Brothers William Howard Flowers and Joseph Hampton Flowers had one goal in mind when they started a small bakery in 1919: providing fresh bread to Thomasville residents. Today, Flowers Foods, famous for its "Little Miss Sunbeam" logo on Sunbeam bread, is one of the largest producers of baked goods in the country, its annual sales totaling more than $1.5 billion.

If you've bought any pecans grown in Georgia, chances are good they came from the South Georgia Pecan Company. The second-largest pecan-shelling company in the country processes more than 50 million pounds of pecans every year. The company was founded by the Pearlman family in Valdosta in 1905 and sold to Beatrice Foods in 1967. In 1983, Ed Crane and Jim Wom took over the company. After the pecans have been shelled and shipped, the empty shells are ground and sold to manufacturers that combine them with resin to make a woodlike product for furniture and building materials.

And let's not forget peanuts, or "goober peas." Georgia produces more peanuts than any other state. Its 755,000 acres of peanut fields yield more than

Peanuts being harvested
GEORGIA DEPARTMENT OF ECONOMIC DEVELOPMENT

2 billion pounds a year. Peanuts are grown mostly in the sandy soil and warm climate of the Coastal Plain.

Although Georgia is known as "the Peach State," two other states—South Carolina and California—actually have more peach orchards. Still, Georgia produces in excess of 2.5 million bushels every year. The Franciscan monks who came to Georgia with the Spanish introduced peaches in 1571 and taught the Cherokees how to grow them. In the 1850s, Raphael Moses of Columbus became one of the first men to profitably ship peaches to other states.

Mining

Georgia is not known for being a mining state, but it did have a brief period of gold fever when the precious metal was discovered in Lumpkin County. The county seat, Licklog, was renamed Dahlonega in 1833 for the Cherokee word *tahlonega*, or "golden." Most of the mining was of the "placer" variety, in which prospectors sifted through the sand and gravel in creeks for gold. Later, mine tunnels were dug into the hills in search of veins of gold.

Gold was so plentiful for a while that Congress authorized the establishment of a mint at Dahlonega to make gold coins. When it closed at the beginning of the Civil War, the mint had produced 1.5 million coins.

While gold meant prosperity to some, it brought only misery and heartbreak to the Cherokees who had owned the land. With the exception of a few who fled to North Carolina to hide in the mountains, the Cherokees were removed and sent to Oklahoma on the Trail of Tears.

Just after the Cherokees were removed, the gold began to run out. A new strike in California in 1849 attracted thousands of Georgians harboring dreams of gold and glory. Most would have settled for gold.

In the 20th century, enough gold was still left in Dahlonega to refurbish the gold dome of the State Capitol in Atlanta.

One of the most profitable mining operations in Georgia today is for "white gold," or kaolin. Georgia is the largest kaolin producer in the country, mining some 8 million tons of the white clay every year. Found in the part of Georgia below the fall line, kaolin is used as a paper coating, in pharmaceuticals, and in ceramics and paints.

Granite is another natural resource that has been extremely profitable for Georgia. Elberton, in the northeastern part of the state, is known as "the granite capital of the world." Forty-five quarries produce rough blocks of granite that are sent to manufacturing plants for grave markers, memorials, and building products such as granite countertops.

Marble is quarried in the town of Tate in Pickens County. Georgia marble has been used all over the world and in 60 percent of the monuments in Washington, D.C. The original Georgia Marble Company, bought and resold several times, is now owned by the Canadian company Polycor. Its United States headquarters is located in Tate.

Timber

The timber industry has been part of Georgia's economy ever since the first settlers set up sawmills to send lumber to England.

What is now Georgia-Pacific began as a small lumber company in Augusta in 1927. Twenty years later, the Georgia Hardwood Lumber Company became Georgia-Pacific Plywood and Lumber Company. Koch Industries acquired Georgia-Pacific for $21 billion in 2005. Georgia-Pacific is the second-largest producer of paper products in North America and the largest supplier of building products. The company has more than 600 facilities in the United States and other countries.

Folks who happen to drive along the coast near Savannah sometimes get a whiff of an odor like rotten eggs. The scent may be unpleasant to tourists, but residents consider it the sweet smell of success. Union Camp turns forest products into pulp, paper, bags, and packaging materials. The Savannah plant, the largest of the New Jersey–based company's facilities, manufactures more than a million tons of paper products every year.

Aerospace and Transportation

Atlanta not only has one of the busiest airports on the planet, it will be home to the world's largest airline once all the legal documents have been signed for the merger of Delta Air Lines with Northwest Airlines. Not bad for a company that began as an aerial crop-dusting outfit in Macon in 1924. Huff Daland Dusters was renamed Delta Air Service after the company moved to Monroe, Louisiana. New owner C. E. Woolman named the company after the Mississippi Delta. The airline moved its headquarters to Atlanta in 1941. Delta long has been one of Atlanta's major employers, but rising fuel costs and other factors forced the airline into bankruptcy and resulted in layoffs a few years ago. It emerged successfully in 2007 by restructuring and downsizing. Now, with the Northwest merger and the expansion of flights to Beijing, China, and other international cities, Delta expects to weather the fuel crisis and return to profitability.

United Parcel Service (UPS) began in Seattle but moved its headquarters to Atlanta in 1991. UPS is a multibillion-dollar corporation that delivers more than 13 million packages worldwide every day. The company has a fleet of 88,000 vehicles and 360,000 employees.

Savannah-based Gulfstream Aerospace Corporation, a subsidiary of General Dynamics, produces aircraft for corporations and private individuals in the United States, Europe, Asia, and the Middle East. Gulfstream planes

UPS planes
GEORGIA DEPARTMENT OF ECONOMIC DEVELOPMENT

range in price from $11 million to $46 million. The planned expansion of the Savannah plant is expected to add 1,100 new jobs by 2013.

Retail

Since beginning with two stores in Atlanta in 1978, The Home Depot has grown into the world's largest home improvement center. The company now operates stores in Canada, Mexico, Chile, and every state in the union. The Home Depot was founded by Bernie Marcus and Arthur Blank after the two men were fired on the same day by Handy Dan Home Improvement Centers in California. The unemployed executives got together to create a plan for a chain of home improvement warehouses that would offer hardware, lumber, and building supplies to both contractors and average consumers. By 2004, sales had reached $60 billion. Marcus and Blank have since retired to devote their time to philanthropic interests. Blank also bought the Atlanta Falcons pro football franchise.

Health and Medicine

The Centers for Disease Control and Prevention (CDC) in Atlanta is world-famous for its efforts in controlling infectious diseases and preventing epidemics. As part of the United States Department of Health and Human Resources, the CDC has a mission that includes vaccinations, nutrition, and family-planning programs around the world. The CDC played a key role in the eradication of smallpox and the identification of the Ebola virus. Today, it has the added responsibility of combating bioterrorism, such as the use of anthrax and other potential biological weapons.

Researcher at The Centers for Disease Control and Prevention
GEORGIA DEPARTMENT OF ECONOMIC DEVELOPMENT

Hollywood Goes South

For a while beginning in the 1970s, it looked like Georgia might become a haven for Hollywood filmmakers. Geographically, the state had everything—mountains, urban centers, islands, beaches, swamps, forests, and vast fields. If the film folks needed a plantation house, we had plantation houses. Looking for a weathered, unpainted shack? We had plenty of those. Need a wild and scenic river where four middle-aged canoeists could test their survival skills? How about the Chattooga?

The film and video industry has contributed more than $5 billion to the state's economy since the Georgia Film Commission was established in 1973. That's a hefty amount, but Georgia has not succeeded as well as North Carolina and other places. In an effort to make Georgia more attractive to movie and television producers, Governor Sonny Perdue signed the 2008 Entertainment Industry Investment Act. The act provides a 20 percent tax credit for certain productions and another 10 percent tax credit if a Georgia logo is used in the film or video.

In 2008, the state reported 279 total entertainment productions, including 10 feature films, 46 television programs and series episodes, 171 commercials, 44 music videos, and eight video game projects.

More than 400 motion pictures and countless TV movies and shows have been made in Georgia, but most are not about Georgia. *Gone With the Wind*, the movie most people associate with Georgia, was filmed on a set in Hollywood. An ample amount of Georgia's red clay was transported there, however.

Movies not only boost the economy of the location where they're shot, they also create longer-lasting benefits. *Deliverance*, shot on the Chattooga River in Rabun County, sparked a huge interest in whitewater canoeing and tourism in the North Georgia mountains. The film *Midnight in the Garden of Good and Evil*, along with the best-selling book by John Berendt, increased tourism in Savannah by an estimated 60 percent. *Fried Green Tomatoes* turned the tiny town of Juliette into a major destination for tourists who wanted to sample the vegetarian delicacy at the Whistle Stop Café. The jobs the movie and TV companies create while they're shooting on location are another positive side effect.

Not all the films made in Georgia have been award winners, and not all have portrayed the state in a favorable light. *Deliverance* angered some of the mountain people of Rabun County because it presented them as ignorant and inbred, not to mention perverted. The 1932 film *I Am a Fugitive from a Chain*

Gang created a national outcry that resulted in prison reform legislation in Georgia. *Smokey and the Bandit* and several other Burt Reynolds movies did little to improve the state's image in the eyes of the rest of the country.

On the other hand, Georgia can be proud of *Driving Miss Daisy*, the Academy Award–winning film about an Atlanta Jewish woman and her black chauffeur; *Glory,* the Civil War film starring Denzel Washington; and *Daughters of the Dust*, a story of an African-American Gullah community on the sea islands in 1902.

Tourism

Tourism continues to be Georgia's second-largest industry. Georgia is the seventh-most-visited state in the country. Every year, 48 million visitors spend about $25 billion at hotels, restaurants, parks, and other places. New attractions such as the Georgia Aquarium and the New World of Coca-Cola in Atlanta and the Georgia Music Hall of Fame and the Georgia Sports Hall of Fame in Macon are expected to boost tourism even more.

Savannah, of course, will continue to ride the wave of national and international publicity generated by *Midnight in the Garden of Good and Evil.*

Top 10 Fortune 500 Companies in Georgia

1. Home Depot (www.homedepot.com)
2. United Parcel Service (www.ups.com)
3. Coca-Cola (www.thecoca-colacompany.com)
4. Coca-Cola Enterprises (www.cokecce.com)
5. Delta Air Lines (www.delta.com)
6. Aflac (www.aflac.com)
7. Southern (www.southerncompany.com)
8. SunTrust Banks (www.suntrust.com)
9. Genuine Parts (www.genpt.com)
10. Mohawk Industries (www.mohawkind.com)

BOOKS AND RESOURCES

Dabney, Joseph Earl. *Herk: Hero of the Skies*. Fairview, N.C.: Bright Mountain Books, 2003.

Georgia Department of Economic Development. www.georgia.org.

New Georgia Encyclopedia. www.georgiaencyclopedia.org.

Sports

NASCAR
GEORGIA DEPARTMENT OF ECONOMIC DEVELOPMENT

In Georgia, like most of the South, college football is not a sport; it's a religion. Yes, we manage to fill the stadiums and arenas for the Atlanta Braves, Hawks, Falcons, and Thrashers, and we pack the stands on NASCAR weekends, but true believers would not be caught dead anywhere but on a college campus when the Bulldogs or the Yellow Jackets or their favorite out-of-state teams are playing. Believe it or not, Georgia is home to alumni and alumnae from Clemson, Auburn, Florida, Duke, Wake Forest, Alabama, Tennessee, Louisiana State, and other schools besides Georgia Tech and the University of Georgia. Rumor has it that even some Notre Dame and Michigan fans are mixed in with the population.

Newcomers who are football and basketball fans get a bonus when they move to the state. If they're Atlantic Coast Conference (ACC) fans, they can go to Georgia Tech games. If they're die-hard Southeastern Conference (SEC) fans, there's the University of Georgia. Both Tech and Georgia have won national championships in football.

Each year, Atlanta is host to the SEC championship football and basketball games and the Chick-fil-A Peach Bowl, which pits an ACC team against an SEC team.

And if you prefer other athletic events, don't worry. You can find almost any sport in Georgia, from tennis and golf to polo and ice hockey.

Atlanta has the big professional teams, including the Atlanta Dream of the Women's National Basketball Association, but baseball fans soon will be able to watch tomorrow's stars on the Gwinnett Braves AAA team at its new, intimate stadium.

Those who enjoy the roar of high-powered engines and the smell of gasoline fumes can head to the Atlanta Motor Speedway for one of the Sprint Cup races (including the Pep Boys Auto 500), Nationwide series races, Camping World truck series races, Legends races, or drag-racing events.

Golf enthusiasts can watch the best players in the world compete at the Masters Tournament in Augusta in April or the AT&T Classic in Duluth. AT&T tickets are easier to get than ones to the Masters. Only those who have inherited Masters tickets from relatives or who are willing to pay thousands of dollars to online sellers are allowed to tread the hallowed ground where Arnold Palmer, Ben Hogan, Sam Snead, Jack Nicklaus, Tiger Woods, and other greats have competed for the famous green jacket.

No matter which sport you love, you can learn about the state's legendary athletes, past and present, at the Georgia Sports Hall of Fame in Macon. More than 300 inductees are represented in exhibits, including baseball greats Ty Cobb and Hank Aaron, football figures John Heisman and Herschel Walker, NASCAR's Bill Elliott, and golf champion Bobby Jones.

College Sports

Georgia Tech

Georgia Tech football teams have not fared well in the past few years against their in-state rivals, the University of Georgia Bulldogs, but the Yellow Jackets have a proud history dating back to 1892. A member of the Atlantic Coast Conference, the Yellow Jackets (also known as the Ramblin' Wreck) play their home games at Bobby Dodd Stadium at historic Grant Field in Atlanta.

Tech has won four national championships and 15 conference titles in football and still holds the record for the most lopsided victory in college football, a 222–0 win over Cumberland College in 1916.

The school has produced a number of coaching legends.

John Heisman, the man for whom the vaunted Heisman Trophy was named, coached Tech in the early years.

William Alexander, who became head coach in 1920, led Tech to a national championship in 1928, the Rose Bowl in 1929, the Orange Bowl in 1940, the Cotton Bowl in 1943, and the Sugar Bowl in 1944.

Bobby Dodd, for whom the stadium is named, led Tech to eight straight victories over UGA, its longest winning streak against the Bulldogs. In 1952, Dodd coached the Yellow Jackets to a perfect 12–0 season (including a Sugar Bowl win over the University of Mississippi) and a national title. Dodd was responsible for Tech's withdrawing from the SEC in 1963 and joining the ACC.

The coaches who followed Dodd did not live up to Tech fans' expectations. Finally, they pinned their hopes on Bobby Ross, who had coached the University of Maryland to three ACC titles. In 1990, Ross coached the team to an 11–0–1 season, a 45–21 victory over Nebraska in the Citrus Bowl, and a share of the national championship.

George O'Leary coached Tech to several winning seasons after Ross's replacement, Bill Lewis, was fired. O'Leary left in 2001 to take the head coaching job at Notre Dame, but the offer was rescinded after some fabrications were discovered in his résumé.

Chan Gailey's arrival in 2002 sparked Tech fans' hopes of a return to the glory of Bobby Dodd's days. Gailey had a couple of seven-win seasons before getting nine victories and the ACC championship in 2006. Gailey was fired in 2007 and replaced by Paul Johnson of Georgia Southern.

Georgia Tech has excelled in other sports as well. In 1985, coach Bobby Cremins led a team starring Mark Price, John Salley, and Bruce Dalrymple to Tech's first ACC championship and to the Elite Eight in the NCAA tournament. Tech made it to the NCAA tournament nine straight times under Cremins, who became the school's most successful basketball coach, claiming 354 wins against 237 losses. Cremins's successor, Paul Hewitt, led Tech to the 2004 NCAA Final Four before losing to the University of Connecticut.

Tech's baseball team, under coach Danny Hall, has advanced to three College World Series and won four ACC regular-season titles and three ACC tournament titles. Tech players who have made it to the major leagues include Nomar Garciaparra, Kevin Brown, Mark Teixeira, and Jason Varitek.

University of Georgia

The University of Georgia Bulldogs have won 35 national championships in baseball, football, golf, equestrian competition, gymnastics, swimming and diving, and tennis. They have also won 128 Southeastern Conference championships in various sports. But the sport that counts most in the hearts of Dawg fans is football.

Georgia football fans have always been loyal, but their enthusiasm reached a fever pitch during the Herschel Walker days, when the Heisman Trophy winner led the Bulldogs to a national championship in 1980. Bulldog Nation has yearned for another national title ever since. Only a series of defeats to the Florida Gators under Coach Steve Spurrier and a few other unexpected losses have kept them from the elusive goal.

UGA has been fielding a football team since 1892. Its coaches have included Glenn "Pop" Warner, George Woodruff, Harry Mehre, Wally Butts, Vince Dooley, Ray Goff, Jim Donnan, and Mark Richt. Butts, who coached from 1939 to 1960, led the team to its first consensus NCAA 1-A national championship in 1942, following a 9–0 victory over UCLA in the Rose Bowl. Star players on that team included Charley Trippi and Frank Sinkwich. The Bulldogs finished first in one national poll in 1946.

Dooley, who served as head coach from 1964 to 1988, led the team to six SEC titles and a national championship in 1980, when the Bulldogs defeated Notre Dame 17–10 in the Sugar Bowl. Star players on that team were Herschel Walker, Buck Belue, and Lindsay Scott. Dooley, who held the post longer than any other Georgia coach, finished with a 201–77–10 record.

Under current coach Mark Richt, Georgia has won two SEC championships and three SEC East Division championships. The Bulldogs defeated Hawaii 41–10 in the 2008 Sugar Bowl. Richt began the 2008–2009 season with a record of 72–19.

Georgia Southern University

When Dale Lick took over as president of this small Statesboro college in 1978, he realized something was missing: a football team. The school had fielded something resembling a team from 1924 to 1941. The Blue Tide, as they were known then, had only four winning seasons.

Lick reinstituted football and jump-started the Georgia Southern Eagles by hiring Erskine "Erk" Russell, a UGA defensive coach, to run the team. Competing against other NCAA 1-AA teams, the Eagles won six national championships between 1985 and 2000. The 1989 team, the last coached by Russell, finished the season at 15–0.

Chipper Jones of the Atlanta Braves
GEORGIA DEPARTMENT OF ECONOMIC DEVELOPMENT

Major Professional Sports

Atlanta Braves

The Braves have been called "America's Team" because their games were televised nationwide via satellite on Ted Turner's "Superstation," WTBS, in the days before widespread cable channels.

The oldest continuously operating sports franchise in America, the Braves began in Boston as the Red Stockings in 1871. The name was changed to the Beaneaters, Doves, Rustlers, Bees, and, finally, Braves. The team moved to Milwaukee in the 1950s and to Atlanta in 1966.

The Braves struggled over the next 25 years. During the team's dismal seasons, embittered fans sometimes stuck their unused tickets under the wiper blades of parked cars. Getting a choice seat behind home plate was not difficult.

One bright spot was the historic night in 1973 when Hank Aaron broke Babe Ruth's record by hitting his 715th home run. For a brief moment, Atlanta baseball fans had something to brag about.

Things began to change for the better in 1991, when the "Miracle Braves" went from worst to first and won the National League pennant. The Braves then went on a streak that included a World Series championship over the Cleveland Indians in 1995.

Atlanta's vaunted pitching staff was the key to its success. In 1995, Greg Maddux won a fourth straight Cy Young Award, boasting a 19–2 record and an earned run average of 1.63. Mark Wohlers was a dominant closer, earning 25 saves. Braves hitters came through at the plate as well. Four players hit more than 20 home runs that year. Fred McGriff had 27; David Justice, 24; Ryan Klesko, 24; and rookie Chipper Jones, 23. In the final game of the World Series, Tom Glavine pitched eight innings and David Justice hit a home run to win the game 1–0.

No parade had welcomed the Braves when they arrived from Milwaukee in 1966, but hundreds of thousands lined the streets of Atlanta to cheer them as World Series champions.

The Braves continued their winning ways into the 21st century but never won a World Series again. Fans still pack the current stadium, Turner Field, to watch new stars Jeff Francoeur and Brian McCann play on the same field with Chipper Jones, John Smoltz, and Tom Glavine. They watch with dreams of the team's glory years and the hope that this season, or maybe next season, will be the one.

Atlanta Falcons

The Falcons made headlines in 2007, but not for anything they did on the playing field. After weeks of rumors, the team's star quarterback, Michael Vick, was suspended for illegal dog-fighting activities on property he owned in Virginia. After Vick was sentenced to prison for 23 months, the Falcons tried to fill the huge vacancy he left with backup quarterbacks.

The Falcons franchise has had a spotty record since the team was formed in 1965 under owner Rankin Smith. Tommy Nobis of the University of Texas became the first Falcon when he was chosen as the number-one pick in the 1966 NFL draft. The team won one game the first season and only 12 during the 1960s.

The Falcons finally made the postseason in 1978 but lost to the Dallas Cowboys in the divisional playoffs. They were back in the playoffs again in 1980 and 1982.

The Falcons had their best season in 1998 when, led by quarterback Chris Chandler, they upset the Minnesota Vikings for the NFC championship and headed for Super Bowl XXXIII. The miracle season ended with a 34–19 loss to the Denver Broncos.

Things began to look up in 2001 with the drafting of Vick from Virginia Tech. A scrambling, agile runner, Vick led the Falcons to the playoffs in 2002, when the team lost to the Philadelphia Eagles.

Bad luck reappeared when Vick broke his leg in the 2003 preseason and missed the first 12 games of the regular schedule. He returned the next year to lead the Falcons to an 11–5 record and another appearance in the playoffs. Once again, they lost to the Philadelphia Eagles.

Georgia Dome
GEORGIA DEPARTMENT OF
ECONOMIC DEVELOPMENT

Things continued to go downhill in 2005 and 2006 with records of 8–8 and 7–9. Then the bottom fell out when Vick was suspended and sent to prison. Coach Jim Mora was fired, and Bobby Petrino was brought in as his replacement. But Petrino abruptly resigned after 13 games to take the head coaching job at the University of Arkansas. Emmitt Thomas, the Falcons' secondary coach, took over as head coach for the final three games.

In January 2008, Mike Smith, a defensive coach for the Jacksonville Jaguars, was hired as head coach. That April, the team drafted Boston College quarterback Matt Ryan. With a new coach and a promising young quarterback, Falcons owner Arthur Blank has promised fans an improved team. Die-hard Falcons supporters are optimistic. The rest of us will believe it when we see it.

Atlanta Hawks

Like the Braves, the Hawks began in another city and eventually moved to Atlanta. The team was born as the Tri-Cities Blackhawks in 1946 and became the Milwaukee Hawks in 1951. In 1955, it moved to St. Louis and stayed for 13 seasons as one of the NBA's top teams, featuring superstars such as Bob Petit. Atlanta became the team's nesting place in 1968 after St. Louis officials refused to build a new arena. The team played for four seasons at Georgia Tech's Alexander Memorial Stadium while the Omni Coliseum was under construction.

The Hawks began their stay in Atlanta with some top talent. Pistol Pete Maravich dazzled the crowds with his fancy dribbling and shooting. Teammate Lou Hudson was a solid superstar.

Ted Turner, owner of the Braves, purchased the Hawks in 1976 and brought in Hubie Brown as head coach. Four years later, the Hawks won the NBA's Central Division. Following the addition of Dominique Wilkins and the hiring of Mike Fratello as coach in 1982, the Hawks became one of the NBA's best teams. They were good, but not good enough to win it all, however, so Lenny Wilkins was hired to replace Fratello in 1993.

In 1994, Hawks management infuriated the fans by trading Dominique Wilkins, a crowd favorite and the franchise's leading all-time scorer. Wilkins's replacement, Danny Manning, left the team at the end of the season. After that disastrous trade and another season in which the Hawks failed to advance in the playoffs, many fans drifted away. Others accepted the notion that the Hawks were never going to make it to the NBA finals.

Time Warner obtained the team in 1996, during its merger with Turner Broadcasting. The Hawks had a new home in Philips Arena, but the change of venue didn't help them much. In 2004, a group of executives bought the Hawks from Time Warner. The new ownership failed to energize the team, which finished the season with only 13 victories. By 2007, the Hawks had played the most consecutive seasons of any NBA team without making the playoffs.

The acquisition of Mike Bibby from the Sacramento Kings in 2008 helped the Hawks make the playoffs for the first time since 1999. Although the team had only a 37–45 record, it took the Boston Celtics to a seventh game in the playoffs, stirring hope among fans for a better season in 2008–2009.

Atlanta Thrashers

Yes, Hotlanta has a professional ice hockey team. In 1997, the Atlanta Thrashers (named after the state bird, the brown thrasher) filled the void left by the Flames when that team left for Calgary in 1980. The Thrashers played their first NHL game in Philips Arena on October 2, 1999, losing 4–1 to the New Jersey Devils.

Owner Time Warner sold the Thrashers (and the Hawks) to a group of investors named Atlanta Spirit, LLC, on September 21, 2003. Eight days later, star forward Dany Heatley and center Dan Snyder were seriously injured when Heatley crashed his Ferrari. Snyder died six days later.

In memory of Snyder, the team wore black uniform patches bearing his number, 37. Heatley was traded to Ottawa at the end of the season for Marian Hossa. In 2007, Hossa, an outstanding offensive player, became the first Thrasher to score 100 points in a season. That same season, the Thrashers won the first division championship in franchise history and landed a spot in the Stanley Cup playoffs for the first time. Unfortunately for the team and the fans, the New York Rangers swept the Thrashers in four games.

Atlanta Dream

Georgia's first Women's National Basketball Association team, the Atlanta Dream, began its inaugural season in 2008. The team, coached by Marynell Meadors, plays its games in Philips Arena.

Golf

Every golf fan knows that Georgia is famous for the Masters and Bobby Jones. The Masters, played every April at Augusta National Golf Club, is one of four major championships in men's professional golf. It is arguably the most prestigious golf tournament in the world, and Jones is arguably one of the greatest champions the game has produced.

Jones and Clifford Roberts started the Masters. Jones created Augusta National Golf Club as a place to play after he retired. He and Roberts found some land in Augusta that seemed perfect for a golf course. Alister MacKenzie was hired to design the course in 1931, and Augusta National officially opened in 1933. The following year, Horton Smith won the first Masters, originally called the Augusta National Invitation Tournament.

The course was closed to golfers and used as a place to raise cattle and turkeys during World War II.

Augusta National and the Masters became famous in the 1960s and 1970s as the battleground of Arnold Palmer, Jack Nicklaus, and Gary Player. Those golfing giants won 11 times in 18 years.

Lee Elder became the first African-American to qualify for the tournament in 1975, but it would be another 15 years before Augusta National admitted a black member. Nicklaus set the record of being the oldest player to win the Masters with his victory in 1986 at the age of 46.

Augusta National became the center of controversy in 2003 when Martha Burk criticized the club for not allowing female members. Though the protest generated national publicity, the club refused to change its policy, and the Masters was played as scheduled.

If the 1960s and 1970s were the era of Palmer, Player, and Nicklaus, the era of the Tiger began in 1997 when Tiger Woods won his first Masters at the age of 21. He won his fourth straight major championship at Augusta National in 2001 and earned the prestigious green jacket again in 2002 and 2005.

Bobby Jones (1902–1971) is not only an icon to Georgia golfers but the

Golf on St. Simons
GEORGIA DEPARTMENT OF ECONOMIC DEVELOPMENT

greatest amateur golfer in history. Born in Atlanta, Jones grew up at a time when golf was a sport gentlemen played for the honor of winning, not for money—at least not for the hundreds of thousands of dollars professional golfers play for today.

An attorney by profession, Jones won 13 major championships in the 1920s, including three British Opens, four United States Opens, five United States Amateurs, and one British Amateur. He was the only golfer to win four major titles—the Grand Slam—in one season. Jones retired at the peak of his game at the age of 28.

Like Tiger Woods today, Jones inspired a generation of young golfers. One of them, Tommy Aaron of Gainesville, began playing at the age of 12. Aaron won the Masters in 1973 and was inducted into the Georgia Sports Hall of Fame in 1979.

Larry Nelson, a native of Alabama who grew up in Georgia, was a successful professional golfer as well. Nelson won the 1981 and 1987 PGA Championships and the 1983 United States Open and played on three Ryder Cup teams. He is a member of the Georgia Golf Hall of Fame and the World Golf Hall of Fame.

As a golfer at the University of North Carolina, Davis Love III of Sea Island was a three-time All-American who won the 1984 ACC tournament championship. Since turning professional, Love has won 18 PGA tournaments. He finished second at the 1995 Masters. Love was inducted into the Georgia Golf Hall of Fame in 2001.

Georgia also has produced some excellent female golfers.

Golf at Callaway Gardens
GEORGIA DEPARTMENT OF ECONOMIC DEVELOPMENT

Louise Suggs, born in Atlanta in 1923, began playing when she was 10. She won several amateur championships, including the North-South Tournament and the United States Amateur. Suggs won the 1949 United States Open in the year that the Women's Professional Golf Association went out of business. She then joined a dozen other female players to form the Ladies Professional Golf Association in 1950.

Long before Tiger Woods charmed the media with his success at a young age, Dot Kirby (1926–2000) was setting a record in Georgia as the youngest golfer to win a state championship. She was 13. Like Bobby Jones, Kirby never turned professional. Golf was a game she played for fun. Kirby won the Georgia State Women's Championship five consecutive times, two National Titleholders Championships, and the 1951 United States Amateur. Kirby was inducted into the Georgia Golf Hall of Fame in 1989.

STOCK CAR RACING

Although Georgia does not have North Carolina's storied history of stock car racing, some believe the seeds of the sport were planted in Dawsonville. Every racing fan today knows that Bill Elliott, nicknamed "Awesome Bill from Dawsonville," is a native of the North Georgia town, but many may not be aware that a Dawsonville liquor-store owner named Raymond Parks was responsible for launching the careers of early drivers.

Stock car historians have confirmed that some of the best drivers have been moonshine runners. Two of these, Roy Hall and Lloyd Seay, were cousins of Parks who persuaded the liquor merchant to finance their careers. Parks provided cars fine-tuned by Atlanta mechanic Red Vogt. Hall and Seay burned up the dirt tracks in the years before World War II. Seay was shot to death during an argument with another cousin about a shipment of sugar (presumably for making moonshine), and Hall retired from racing.

Parks and Vogt were among the key players who organized the National Association for Stock Car Auto Racing in Daytona Beach, Florida, in 1947. The Parks-Vogt team launched the careers of Bob and Fonty Flock, Gober Sosebee, Jack Smith, and Red Byron, who won the 1949 NASCAR championship.

The driver best known among contemporary race fans, however, is Bill Elliott, who in 1985 became the first driver to win $1 million in a race. He captured the Winston Cup Championship in 1988.

The only Georgia track still hosting Sprint Cup events is the Atlanta Motor Speedway in Hampton. But Georgia fans think nothing of driving hundreds of miles to NASCAR events all over the South.

Tour de Georgia
GEORGIA DEPARTMENT OF ECONOMIC DEVELOPMENT

Other Sports

Cycling

The Tour de Georgia, a challenging bicycle event modeled on the Tour de France, takes cyclists 600 miles through the state in six days. One of the stages involves a steep climb to the top of Brasstown Bald, Georgia's highest mountain. The race, which has an economic impact of an estimated $38 million on the state, was launched in 2002 by the Georgia Department of Industry and

Trade to benefit the Georgia Cancer Coalition. Funds from the 2008 race were donated to the Aflac Cancer Center and Blood Disorders Service of Children's Healthcare of Atlanta.

Running

Every Fourth of July in Atlanta, more than 50,000 runners (and walkers) line up at the Lenox Mall in what has become the largest 10K road race in the world. The race attracts some 150,000 friends and fans, who line the 6.2-mile course to cheer on their favorites. The *Atlanta-Journal Constitution* Peachtree Road Race 10K started in 1970 with a group of about 100 runners. Winners get prize money, and others get T-shirts. Anyone can participate as long as they turn their applications in by the deadline. For more information, contact the Atlanta Track Club; its website is www.atlantatrackclub.org.

Books and Resources

Green, Ron, Sr. *The Masters: 101 Reasons to Love Golf's Greatest Tournament.* Stewart, Tabori & Chang, 2008.

New Georgia Encyclopedia. www.georgiaencyclopedia.org.

Rapoport, Ron. *The Immortal Bobby: Bobby Jones and the Golden Age of Golf.* New York: Wiley, 2005.

Smith, Loren. *The University of Georgia Football Vault.* Whitman Publishing, 2007.

Wilkinson, Jack. *Georgia Tech Football Vault.* Whitman Publishing, 2008.

Travel and Leisure

Rafting on the Chattooga River
GEORGIA DEPARTMENT OF ECONOMIC DEVELOPMENT

If you're a newcomer to Georgia, you already may be overwhelmed by how many travel and recreation opportunities the state offers. You're probably overwhelmed by the traffic in Atlanta, too, but there's nothing anyone can do about that other than suggesting you take MARTA, the public rail and bus system. What *will* help is a sampling of places to visit and activities and festivals to attend.

This is by no means a complete guide. The many other books on that subject include the *Georgia Travel Guide*, the official state publication, available by clicking on the "Travel" section at www.georgia.org. Individual county chambers of commerce offer brochures and information about things to do in their areas.

What follows is a description of some of the state's most popular attractions, museums, recreational activities, and state parks. Because Georgia has such a diverse geography, it offers something for everyone.

Those who love fishing, boating, or any kind of watersport will find plenty of opportunities to get wet. In North Georgia, canoeists, rafters, and kayakers can test their skills on the wild and scenic Chattooga River or the Coosawattee River. The state has an abundance of lakes, including Carters, Lanier, Oconee, West Point, Sinclair, Seminole, Walter F. George, and Allatoona. Lake Hartwell, Russell Lake, and Clarks Hill Lake—three large reservoirs on the Savannah River—are considered a fisherman's paradise.

People who would rather have their hair set on fire than spend a night in a tent or cabin in the woods can find more than enough arts and culture in Atlanta, Savannah, Augusta, Macon, Columbus, and other metropolitan areas to fill their social calendars. And folks who prefer the great outdoors to symphony halls and museums have their choice of hiking or camping in the mountains or on an island on the Georgia coast. And if you desire to mingle with alligators and observe bird life, you can visit the Okefenokee Swamp—or the Okefenokee National Wildlife Refuge, as it's officially called.

Georgia is a place where the Old South and the New South coexist. Fans of *Gone With the Wind* can go looking for Tara (or plantation houses that inspired Margaret Mitchell). History buffs can explore the archaeological sites of previous civilizations and visit battlefields, forts, and Civil War museums.

Those who couldn't care less about history can revel in modern cityscapes, cheer on their favorite college or pro sports team, listen to the latest rock, rap, or bluegrass band in concert, or enjoy a dazzling variety of global cuisine, from French and Italian to Thai and Latin. In Georgia, you're likely to find a sushi bar just down the street from a catfish restaurant, or a Mexican cantina three doors up from a rib shack.

The important thing is to get out of the house or apartment as often as you can to explore this magnificent state. Sadly, some natives and longtime residents have never attended a performance of *Swamp Gravy*, pigged out at the Big Pig Jig, or nibbled a reptile appetizer at the Whigham Rattlesnake Roundup. Do you really want to die without climbing Stone Mountain or taking a boat tour through the Okefenokee Swamp? Well, maybe so, but everyone should make their own bucket list for Georgia before they, well, kick the bucket.

Not only will you learn about Georgia by traveling from Rabun Gap to Tybee Light and visiting as many of the 159 counties as you can, you also will learn about the people. And as you'll soon discover, some of the people are far more interesting than anything you'll find in a museum.

Northeastern Georgia

The foothills of the Appalachian Mountains begin about an hour's drive north of Atlanta. After another 30 or 40 minutes, you'll find yourself looking up at a range of majestic peaks. Here, you can climb to the top of Brasstown Bald, Georgia's highest mountain, sit and gaze in wonder at Amicalola Falls, go trout fishing during the season, book a rafting trip on the Chattooga River, or take a 10-mile hike from Unicoi Gap to Tray Mountain. Ambitious hikers can begin the 2,144-mile trek along the Appalachian Trail to Maine.

Gold seekers can try their hand at gem mining in Dahlonega, the site of an early gold rush. If you don't strike it rich, don't worry. You'll find other treasures to savor up here. BlackStock Vineyards, Wolf Mountain Vineyards, Three Sisters Vineyards, Montaluce Winery and Estates, and Frogtown Cellars offer tastings of local wine and bottles of various vintages that you can purchase to take home or carry on a mountain picnic.

One word of caution if you plan to travel to the mountains during leaf season: the roads, especially on weekends, are crowded with thousands of visitors intent on gazing at the fall colors, stocking up on apples and cider from roadside stands, and venturing into Helen, a faux Bavarian village of restaurants, gift shops, and stores selling fudge and funnel cakes. Funnel cakes—fried swirls of dough with powdered sugar—are like beignets, only bigger.

Here are some other places to go and things to see in the northeastern Georgia mountains.

Babyland General Hospital Doll collectors of all ages are drawn to this popular attraction in Cleveland. If you arrive at the right time, you can

witness the "birth" of a Cabbage Patch Kid in an old-fashioned medical clinic. Adoptions complete with "authentic" birth certificates can be arranged.

Bratwurst, Beer, and More   Helen, the aforementioned Bavarian village, features a variety of things to do besides stuffing your face with fudge, funnel cakes, and sausages. Since the town is located on the Chattahoochee River, tubing and swimming are popular warm-weather events at Cool River Tubing, Helen Tubing, and Waterpark. In the fall, Helen hosts Oktoberfest, a celebration that includes substantial beer consumption. Nora's Mill Granary, a restored, working mill on the Chattahoochee, is open for demonstrations and the sale of its stone-ground cornmeal and grits. Unicoi Lodge and State Park is only a few miles away. And for an elegant visit, check out Smithgall Woods Conservation Area and Lodge. Catch-and-release trout fishing, hiking, bicycling, and tours are offered by reservation only. Cottages, rooms at the lodge, and meals are available, also by reservation.

While you're visiting Helen, drive a few miles north on Ga. 255 toward Clarkesville to the Old Sautee Store and Museum. A popular, picturesque tourist spot, the 135-year-old store features nostalgic memorabilia and gifts.

Château Elan Winery and Resort   If you look to your left about an hour's drive north from Atlanta on I-85, you'll see a view that will make you do a double take. Rising out of what probably was once some farmer's pasture is a replica of a 16th-century French château. The surrounding fields are now vineyards, and the château itself houses a winery, a gift shop, a restaurant, and an Irish pub. It is situated next to a 275-room inn with more restaurants, a spa, a golf course, tennis courts, and nature trails. Château Elan founder Donald Panoz and his family also offer a racing school and a course for motorcycle races at Road Atlanta in Braselton.

Elvis   Yes, every rock-'n'-roll fan knows that Elvis Presley has left the building, but some are determined to keep the King's legacy alive. On the third floor of the Loudermilk Boarding House Museum in Cornelia, Joni Mabe has

assembled the Panoramic Encyclopedia of Everything Elvis. Items include an Elvis Wart (I'm not making this up), the "Maybe Elvis Toenail," and the official Elvis Prayer Rug, complete with instructions.

Fishing   Serious anglers can find plenty of lakes and streams in which to dip their bait and lures, but families with children may want to take the easy way out and let the kids fish at one of the pay-per-pound trout farms. Riverside Trout Farm in Clarkesville charges $4 per pound and furnishes equipment for all ages. Rainbow Ranch Trout Farm in Cumming provides equipment and charges $4.49 per pound. At the Lake Burton Trout Hatchery north of Clarkesville, adults can try to hook a brown or rainbow trout while the kids fish in a stocked catfish pond. Two more pay-for-your-catch lakes are Hickorynut Cove Trout Farm and Upper Hightower Trout Farm in Hiawassee. Andy's Trout Farm in Dillard rents cane poles and sells bait to any anglers willing to pay $3.60 per pound for every trout caught. You can get your fish cleaned for a fee. The only rule is, you catch 'em, you keep 'em. No throwing back is allowed.

Gainesville   This is not the Gainesville where the hated (by UGA fans) University of Florida Gators play. This Gainesville, located near Lake Lanier about an hour north of Atlanta, is the gateway to the North Georgia mountains. Attractions in Gainesville include the Brenau University art collection; the Quinlan Visual Arts Center; the Elachee Nature Science Center and its natural history exhibits, hiking trails, native plants, and live animals; and the Northeast Georgia History Center, which features Chief Whitepath's 1870s cabin.

South of Gainesville, Lake Lanier Islands Resort offers two golf courses, a water park, a hotel, a beach, and boat rentals.

Hot Wheels, Hopping Marsupials, and More   Dawsonville has the distinctions of being the home of NASCAR legend Bill Elliott and the location of the largest kangaroo collection outside Australia. You can learn more about

"Awesome Bill from Dawsonville" at Georgia's Racing Hall of Fame, located east of town. As for the kangaroos, you can see them and other exotic animals at the Kangaroo Conservation Center, located at 222 Bailey-Waters Road.

If kangaroos are not exotic enough for you, venture over to Hiawassee to the Crystal River Ranch for a visit with some llamas. Agricultural demonstrations and treks with the llamas are offered. And if you decide a llama would make a wonderful addition to your farm or suburban backyard, you can buy one starting at $500 (for males).

In Royston, Fancy Feather Farms lets visitors get up close and personal with ostriches, emus, and miniature goats. Tours are by appointment. Royston, by the way, was home to baseball legend Ty Cobb. Some of Cobb's memorabilia and photographs are exhibited at the Ty Cobb Museum.

Jefferson Two attractions are worth your while in this town, known as "the birthplace of anesthesia." The Crawford W. Long Museum offers exhibits about the life and career of Dr. Crawford W. Long, who first used ether to perform "painless" surgery on March 30, 1842, in Jefferson. You can continue your educational tour with a visit to Shields-Etheridge Heritage Farm, an outdoor agricultural museum with a gristmill, a restored schoolhouse from the early 1900s, a cotton gin, and a blacksmith shop.

Pottery and Crafts You can find handcrafted pottery at most galleries in North Georgia. In addition, you can see the artists' works in their studios during the Mountain Heritage Arts Tour, held the last weekend in June. The tour includes the picturesque Mark of the Potter on the Soque River, Hickory Flat Pottery and the Burton Gallery in Clarkesville, and the Folk Pottery Museum in Sautee. The Sautee museum features the work of some of the region's outstanding potters, including Lanier Meaders. More clay products can be seen and purchased at Turpin Pottery in Homer and Crocker Pottery–Georgia Folk Pottery Center in Lula.

Other arts and crafts are on display at the Georgia Heritage Center for the Arts in Tallulah Falls and Clarkesville, Blue Bell Gallery and Bendzunas Glass Studio and Gallery in Comer, and the Funky Chicken Art Project in Dahlonega. And gourds galore are available at The Gourd Place in Sautee. The museum and shop showcase more than 200 gourds from all over the world.

Northwestern Georgia

History buffs and lovers of the outdoors have plenty to see and enjoy in this part of the state. Visitors to Civil War battlefields in Lookout Mountain, Chickamauga, Pickett's Mill, and Allatoona Pass can walk some of the same roads used by Union and Confederate soldiers and view the old trenches and earthworks.

Those interested in earlier periods of history can tour the Etowah Indian Mounds Historic Site and learn about some of the first inhabitants on the continent. The story of the Cherokees and the Trail of Tears is told in exhibits at the Chieftains Museum in Rome. New Echota, the former capital of the Cherokee Nation, is located in Calhoun. Visitors can learn about another interesting chapter in Cherokee history at the Chief Vann House and Museum in Chatsworth. The brick mansion was built in 1804 for James Vann, a controversial half-Scottish, half-Cherokee chief considered one of the richest men in America. He also made a lot of enemies and was murdered by an unknown assailant.

Thanks to Lake Allatoona, Carters Lake, and Lake Blue Ridge, this area has no shortage of fishing and boating opportunities. Hikers and backpackers can challenge themselves on the rugged Cumberland Plateau, where Tennessee, Alabama, and Georgia meet. And the area's deep canyons and limestone caves make it an attractive destination for hang gliders and spelunkers.

More hiking trails are located in the Cloudland Canyon, Red Top Mountain, and Lookout Mountain areas. The Silver Comet Trail, a 37-mile handicapped-accessible paved track between Smyrna and Rockmart, is well used by hikers, roller-bladers, and cyclists (only nonmotorized bikes are allowed).

Northwestern Georgia is one of the most scenic regions in the state, especially along the Lookout Mountain Parkway and the Ridge and Valley Scenic Byway. If you go eastward to Blue Ridge, be sure to take a ride on the Blue Ridge Scenic Railway and treat the family to a movie at the nostalgic 1950s Swan Drive-In Theatre.

Here are a few more highlights.

Apples Galore   You'll find enough apples in Gilmer County to keep doctors away for months. The state's apple capital has 11 orchards along Ga. 52. The town of Ellijay hosts the Apple Festival every fall. Panorama Orchards offers seasonal pick-your-own apples and apple products all year long. Hillcrest Orchards sells sorghum syrup and other farm products, as well as apples. Activities in the fall include wagon rides and a petting zoo.

Barnsley Gardens Resort in Adairsville   The Italianate villa and the surrounding gardens were built by Godfrey Barnsley for his wife, Julia, in the 1840s. A series of tragedies—including Julia's death, damage during the Civil War, and a 1906 tornado—left the once-beautiful estate in ruins. Prince Hubertus Fugger bought the property in 1988 and restored the gardens and the manor house as a resort destination with luxurious cottages.

Cartersville   One must-see attraction is the Booth Western Art Museum, which features an impressive collection of Western and Civil War art. More than 200 paintings and sculptures depict the history and legends of the Old West. One section includes Western movie posters. While you're in Cartersville, stop by the Allatoona Pass Battlefield to see the earthen forts and the miles of trench works where Union and Confederate forces clashed on October 5, 1864. And don't forget the Etowah Indian Mounds Historic Site, where Native Americans lived before 1550 A.D., and Tellus, the Northwest Georgia Science Museum, which offers mineral and fossil exhibits and science experiments.

Flicks under the Stars   If you remember Elvis, you've probably gone to at least one drive-in theater. But you probably haven't seen one like Trenton's Wilderness Outdoor Movie Theater, billed as the world's largest single-screen outdoor movie theater and drive-in. You can watch the film from your car or sit outside on a hillside.

Booth Western Art Museum
GEORGIA DEPARTMENT OF
ECONOMIC DEVELOPMENT

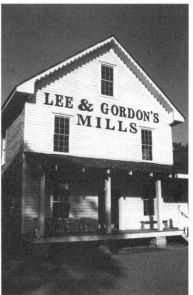

Howard Finster's Vision House   The house in Summerville where folk artist Howard Finster said he received a vision from God to paint sacred art is now a museum and gallery showcasing the late artist's work.

Life on the Farm   You can show the kids where milk comes from and try to find your way through the corn maze at Cagle's Dairy Farm in Canton. Tours of the farm and gardens are available. Nearby Tanglewood Farm Miniatures features more than 100 really small animals, including dwarf bunnies and potbelly pigs. Petting is encouraged.

Peaks and Valleys   Visitors who are not afraid of heights can learn to hang glide at Lookout Mountain Flight Park and Training Center in Rising Fawn. Those who like to keep their feet on the ground can explore along the ridge at Cloudland Canyon State Park or descend to the bottom and look up at the waterfalls.

Pieces of History   In Chickamauga, plan on touring the Gordon-Lee Mansion, an antebellum house used during the Battle of Chickamauga, and the Lee and Gordon Mills, one of the oldest operating mills in the state with one of the oldest general stores. In Dalton, stop and see Prater's Mill, a gristmill built in 1855. A country fair is held here in October. For additional glimpses into the past, visit the Funk Heritage Center and Appalachian Settlement, Georgia's official Frontier and Southeastern Indian Interpretive Center, located in Waleska.

Rock City   Folks who grew up in the South remember seeing red barns with their roofs painted in bold white letters urging travelers to "SEE ROCK

CITY." Today, only a few of those barns are left, and replicas are sold as birdhouses. Well, in Lookout Mountain, you can finally inspect the Rock City Gardens up close. More than 400 species of native plants grow along a path that leads through gardens and rock formations.

Stuffed and Mounted   You can see a large collection of taxidermy at Bud Jones Taxidermy Museum in Tallapoosa. In addition to displays of preserved exotic animals, Jones has an impressive collection of fossils.

Metro Atlanta

Atlanta is a booming city that is the corporate headquarters of Delta Air Lines, UPS, Coca-Cola, CNN, and other companies. It is the home of the Atlanta Braves, the Atlanta Hawks, the Atlanta Falcons, the Atlanta Thrashers, and the Atlanta Dream, a women's professional basketball team.

The city and the surrounding metro area offer all the entertainment you would expect in a large urban center: live theater; art museums; ballet; a symphony orchestra; blues, bluegrass, rap, and rock concerts; and more. You can see pandas at Zoo Atlanta, whale sharks and other denizens of the deep at the Georgia Aquarium, and more than 100 years of Coke memorabilia at the New World of Coca-Cola. Tours are available of CNN's news operation just across from Centennial Olympic Park, a 21-acre green space that features the Olympic Ring Fountain and playgrounds.

History buffs can tour Civil War sites; experience the sights and sounds of the Battle of Atlanta at the Cyclorama; visit Martin Luther King, Jr.'s, birth home and historic Ebenezer Baptist Church, where he first preached; learn more about the historical events in the city's past at the Atlanta History

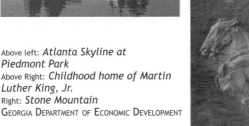

Above left: *Atlanta Skyline at Piedmont Park*
Above Right: *Childhood home of Martin Luther King, Jr.*
Right: *Stone Mountain*
GEORGIA DEPARTMENT OF ECONOMIC DEVELOPMENT

Center; and walk through "The Dump," the house where Margaret Mitchell wrote *Gone With the Wind.*

For family fun, Six Flags Over Georgia offers rides for kids and grownups, including some of the most scream-inducing roller coasters you'll ever climb aboard. East of Atlanta, Stone Mountain Park features scenic train rides, a paddlewheel boat tour, a sky ride to the top of the mountain, campgrounds, and a nightly fireworks and laser light show in front of the giant carvings of Stonewall Jackson, Robert E. Lee, and Jefferson Davis.

And of course, there's shopping. Atlanta is surrounded by malls, but Lenox Square and Phipps Plaza are the most accessible for shoppers staying in the downtown area. If you don't mind driving an hour, you can visit Gwinnett Place Mall, Discover Mills, and the Mall of Georgia, located along I-85 North. Back downtown, souvenir seekers can venture below the city streets to Underground Atlanta for shops, entertainment, dining, and a glimpse of what Atlanta looked like decades ago.

Entire books have been written on the things to do and places to go in Metro Atlanta. The following are a few other highlights.

Atlanta Botanical Garden   Visitors can stop and smell the flowers—and other plants—in this 30-acre garden in midtown Atlanta.

Atlanta History Center   This center features exhibits tracing the city's growth from a small railroad town to a sprawling metropolis. Located on the center's 32 acres of woods and gardens are the Tullie Smith House, an 1840s plantation house typical of upcountry Georgia, and the Swan House, a 1924 mansion built by Atlanta banker Edward Inman. The house is decorated with swans in the woodwork and wallpaper.

Auburn Avenue Historic District   Locally known as "Sweet Auburn," this part of Atlanta was a thriving black entertainment and business district from 1890 until the 1930s. After a period of decline, it has undergone a renewal. Along Auburn Avenue, you'll find Ebenezer Baptist Church, the Martin Luther King Jr. Center for Nonviolent Social Change, and the birthplace of Martin Luther King, Jr.

Chattahoochee River National Recreation Area   Visitors can hike and picnic along the scenic banks of the Chattahoochee.

DeKalb Farmers Market If you're not hungry when you arrive at this gigantic international market in Decatur, you will be before you leave. Fruits, vegetables, fish, and meat from around the world are sold here. You'll hear conversations in more languages than you can identify. A restaurant and bakery are conveniently located in the market.

Fernbank Museum of Natural History   Here, you can feast your eyes on replicas of the giant dinosaurs that once feasted on anything they could catch. Exhibits explain the earth's history. The IMAX theater features breathtaking documentaries on the natural world.

Tullie Smith House
Georgia Department of Economic Development

DeKalb Farmers Market
GEORGIA DEPARTMENT OF ECONOMIC DEVELOPMENT

Fernbank Science Center Not to be confused with the Fernbank Museum, this learning center surrounded by 65 acres of forest features a NASA education lab and a 500-seat planetarium.

Final Resting Places If you're one of those people who like to tour old cemeteries, you'll find unique gravestones at Atlanta's Historic Oakland Cemetery marking the remains of Confederate soldiers, Margaret Mitchell, Bobby Jones, and other notable Atlantans. North of Atlanta, more than 10,000 Civil War soldiers are buried in Marietta National Cemetery. The Marietta Confederate Cemetery/Marietta City Cemetery has graves dating back to the 1830s.

Fox Theatre This 1929 Moorish-Egyptian-style structure, built for the Shriners Club, was turned into a movie theater by film mogul William Fox. Even if you don't go here for one of the summer movies or touring Broadway shows, take a tour just to see the architectural details, including the ceiling with special effects that change the sky from a light blue with clouds to a night scene with stars.

Georgia Aquarium Billed as "the world's largest aquarium," this 8-million-gallon Atlanta fishtank showcases more than 120,000 fish and animals, including whale sharks and penguins.

Georgia State Capitol and Museum Visitors learn about the state's political history from a collection of artifacts and artwork beneath the gold dome.

Gone With the Wind Fans of the book and movie can learn about the author at the Margaret Mitchell House & Museum in Atlanta. Early

Road to Tara Museum
GEORGIA DEPARTMENT OF ECONOMIC
DEVELOPMENT

Wren's Nest House Museum
GEORGIA DEPARTMENT OF ECONOMIC
DEVELOPMENT

photographs and writings are on display, and the restored apartment where she wrote the famous novel is available for tours. You can find more *GWTW* memorabilia at the Road to Tara Museum in Jonesboro and Scarlett on the Square, the Marietta *Gone With the Wind* museum. The Marietta museum has a section devoted to African-American cast members from the film.

High Museum of Art   Here, you can view masterpieces by American and European artists, the impressionists, and folk artists, as well as traveling exhibitions from the Louvre.

Jimmy Carter Library and Museum   The story of the former president's early life and White House years unfolds in a number of exhibits.

New World of Coca-Cola   The history of the world's most famous drink is told in exhibits, films, and a pop culture gallery. The tasting room features 70 different beverages from around the world.

White Water and American Adventures   You can get all wet at this theme park in Marietta featuring water slides, a wave pool, and the Cliffhanger, one of the world's highest free falls.

Wren's Nest House Museum   The home of Joel Chandler Harris, creator of the Uncle Remus tales, is now a museum that offers tours and storytelling.

Zoo Atlanta   Of course, you'll find lions and tigers and bears here, but the pandas from China are the stars of the show.

University of Georgia band
GEORGIA DEPARTMENT OF ECONOMIC DEVELOPMENT

Athens

The "Classic City" is famous as the home of the University of Georgia, R.E.M., and the B-52s. It also is a picturesque city with many antebellum homes. Fortunately for the owners of these mansions, Union general William T. Sherman was too busy burning Atlanta to divert his March to the Sea 65 miles eastward to Athens. One of these grand dwellings is the Taylor-Grady House, the 1844 Greek Revival mansion where *Atlanta Constitution* editor Henry Grady lived while attending college. Tours are available for this as well as the T. R. R. Cobb House, home of the author of the Confederate Constitution, and the 1825 Wray-Nicholson House, which is now the headquarters of the UGA Alumni Association.

Athens has a number of interesting clubs, restaurants, and attractions, but you don't want to visit them on a football weekend—unless you have tickets to the game. No matter who the Bulldogs are playing, more than 92,000 screaming fans pack Sanford Stadium. Those who don't climb into their cars to navigate the traffic jam hang around to patronize the clubs and restaurants downtown.

Besides being a center of sports and music, Athens has become something of a literary town, thanks to the several authors who live in the vicinity and the national reputations of the University of Georgia Press and the *Georgia Review.*

Watkinsville, located eight miles south of Athens on Ga. 441, is a revitalized small town that has become an arts-and-crafts center noted for its antique shops and galleries. The Eagle Tavern, which served as a stagecoach stop in the 19th century, is now a crafts shop and welcome center.

Located 40 miles east of Athens, Washington is a town of about 5,000 that was named for our first president. It features annual tours of antebellum homes, including the white-columned Robert Toombs House. Toombs was the Confederacy's secretary of state for five months. He resigned to serve as a brigadier general in the Army of Northern Virginia.

Augusta Riverwalk

Augusta

Founded as a trading post in 1735 by General James Oglethorpe, this city on the Savannah River is best known as the site of the Masters Tournament at Augusta National Golf Club every April.

The oldest and largest city in this part of the state, Augusta is a place where the Old South meets the New South. Like Athens, Augusta survived the Civil War with most of its historic buildings undamaged. That's the Old South. Part of the city's New South image is represented by Riverwalk, a redeveloped section of antique shops, art galleries, and restaurants along a levee on the Savannah River. The 1886 Cotton Exchange in Riverwalk is a visitor center and museum offering exhibits about the history of the cotton trade in Augusta. Riverwalk is the location of several festivals during the year, including Oktoberfest and the Junior League's Festival of Trees.

Augusta is also the home of the Morris Museum of Art, a facility specializing in Southern art. Its paintings include Southern landscapes, Civil War art, and folk art.

Other points of interest include Artists' Row, a series of shops and studios

Bargain Basement *by Lamar Dodd at the Morris Museum of Art*
GEORGIA DEPARTMENT OF
ECONOMIC DEVELOPMENT

on Broad Street; the Lucy Craft Laney Museum of Black History; the Laney-Walker Historic District; the Sacred Heart Cultural Center, where two of the three Georgia signers of the Declaration of Independence are buried; and Phinizy Swamp Nature Park, which offers trails and observation decks where visitors can watch alligators, hawks, and other wildlife.

Augusta also can claim a connection to two famous individuals in widely different fields. President Woodrow Wilson spent his childhood at a house on Seventh Street, and James Brown, "the Godfather of Soul," learned his music and his moves in Augusta. Check with the Augusta Convention and Visitors Bureau for information about a James Brown tour of 13 special sites.

Savannah and the Coast

Savannah is the oldest city in Georgia—and also arguably the most Irish. On St. Patrick's Day, anyone with the most tenuous connection to Ireland shows up to watch the parade, enjoy the music, and drink green beer. Stay away if you are uncomfortable in crowds. Otherwise, put on your green and join the festivities.

Savannah is both a charmed and a charming city. General Sherman reportedly was so taken by its beauty that he refused to burn the elegant homes. Instead, he presented Savannah to President Abraham Lincoln as a Christmas present.

The city has survived devastating hurricanes, fires, and unbridled growth. While industries and shopping malls have sprung up around Savannah, the

Mercer House in Savannah
GEORGIA DEPARTMENT OF ECONOMIC DEVELOPMENT

downtown, with its moss-draped oaks and shaded streets, has retained the charm of a colonial village.

The one thing Savannah almost didn't survive was the attention it got when a New Yorker named John Berendt decided to write about a scandalous murder trial involving well-known antique dealer Jim Williams. Covering the trial would have been scandalous enough, but Berendt also included detailed portraits of some of Savannah's more, shall we say, "eccentric" characters in *Midnight in the Garden of Good and Evil.*

Other people would have been embarrassed, but the citizens of Savannah opened their arms and their businesses to the flood of tourists that arrived as a result of the best-selling book. Then came the movie, directed by Clint Eastwood. Tourism figures hit the roof.

Now, *Midnight in the Garden of Good and Evil* tours add to an already full slate of things to see and do in Savannah. Among the stops on the *Midnight* tour are the Mercer House on Bull Street, the Italianate mansion where the murder took place; the Hamilton-Turner House on Abercorn Street, the home of Joe Odom, the charming con man in the book; and Bonaventure Cemetery, where the "bird girl" pictured on the cover of *Midnight* resided.

If you drive south from Atlanta along the coast, you eventually will reach St. Simons Island and the Golden Isles. This sparkling necklace of islands has been fought over by Creek and Guale Indians, the Spanish, and the British. Britain finally triumphed in 1742 at the Battle of Bloody Marsh on St. Simons Island.

Cotton and rice planters cultivated the fertile soil of the islands and built great plantation houses during the 18th and 19th centuries. Then, in the late 1800s, Henry Ford and other millionaires bought Jekyll Island and formed the Jekyll Island Club as an exclusive winter resort. The state bought Jekyll in 1947 and opened it to anyone who wanted to play golf or tennis, go biking or hiking along the moss-draped trails, or sunbathe on the white beaches.

Nearby St. Simons Island also offers golf and resort living. Cumberland Island, the southernmost in the chain, is a protected wilderness noted for its wild horses, birds, and other wildlife. Once owned by Thomas Carnegie, brother of Andrew Carnegie, Cumberland is now administered by the National Park Service. It is accessible only by ferry.

Here are some other coastal attractions.

Blackbeard Island Named for famous pirate Edward Teach, this island is now a wildlife refuge offering hiking trails and places for bird watching. It is accessible by a short boat or canoe ride from Sapelo Island.

Butler's Island In 1788, Major Pierce Butler established one of the world's largest rice plantations on this site near Darien. His wife, British actress Fanny Kemble, recorded her critical views of slavery and colonial life in *Journal of a Residence on a Georgian Plantation*.

Hofwyl-Broadfield Plantation Located 78 miles south of Savannah in Brunswick, this rice plantation features educational exhibits, a slide show, and a scenic trail among the rice levees.

Jekyll Island The Georgia Sea Turtle Center has interactive exhibits and demonstrations about turtles. The Jekyll Island Museum and the Jekyll Island Club National Historic Landmark District feature exhibits about the island's history.

Ossabaw Island Georgia's third-largest barrier island offers hiking, camping, and guided tours.

Sapelo Island Visitors can explore Hog Hammock, an African-American Geechee community whose residents are descended from slaves, on this beautiful, unspoiled island. A ferry ride is required to reach Sapelo. Guided tours can be booked through the Sapelo Island Natural Estuarine Research Reserve.

Savannah The best way to see Savannah for the first time is to book one of the many tours. Contact the Savannah Visitors and Convention Bureau (www.savcb.com) for tours and information. If you decide to explore Savannah on your own, your first stop should be River Street, the nine-block stretch along the river with old cotton warehouses that have been converted into shops, pubs, art galleries, hotels, and restaurants. While you're on River Street, stop

St. Simons Lighthouse
GEORGIA DEPARTMENT OF ECONOMIC DEVELOPMENT

at the Ships of the Sea Maritime Museum, housed in the 1819 Scarbrough House. William Scarbrough was one of the financial backers of the *Savannah*, the first steamship to cross the Atlantic. Models of the *Savannah* and other ships, maritime antiques, and memorabilia are exhibited here. And don't miss the *Waving Girl* statue of Florence Martus in Riverfront Plaza. Martus greeted passing ships every day for 50 years. Some say she was awaiting the return of the sailor she loved. Others suggest she did it out of boredom. Savannah offers many excellent dining experiences, including TV chef Paula Deen's Lady & Sons restaurant, at 102 West Congress Street.

St. Simons Island The most prominent landmark on the island is the St. Simons Lighthouse. Visitors can climb to the top for a view of the ocean and the fishing pier at Neptune Park. Tours of the Museum of Coastal History and the Coastal Encounters Nature Center are available.

Tybee Island Georgia's oldest and tallest active lighthouse houses a museum with exhibits about the island's history. Visitors can learn about Georgia's fish and wildlife at the Tybee Island Marine Science Center, which offers aquariums and a touch tank.

Waycross: Obediah's Okefenok, home of "King of the Okefenokee" Obediah Barber, features a variety of native and exotic animals. The Okefenokee Heritage Center offers exhibits on South Georgia history.

Georgia's Heartland

This region south of Atlanta is dotted with picturesque little towns and some of Georgia's most beautiful homes. If you're looking for houses that resemble Tara or Twelve Oaks, you'll find them in the historic town of Madison. Examples include Heritage Hall, a restored 1833 mansion, and the Rogers House, an 1804 Piedmont Plain–style townhouse.

The 1996 Olympic Games were held mainly in Atlanta, but the Georgia International Horse Park in Conyers was the site of the equestrian and mountain-biking events. Visitors today can use the horse and biking trails and attend special events. Conyers also is the home of the Monastery of the Holy Spirit, which includes the Abbey Church, a gift shop, and a bonsai garden. Tours and religious retreats are available.

Eatonton is famous for two authors: Alice Walker and Joel Chandler Harris. Walker, author of *The Color Purple*, grew up here. Harris, who created the Uncle Remus tales about Br'er Rabbit and Br'er Fox, is commemorated in the Uncle Remus Museum. A statue of Br'er Rabbit stands on the courthouse square. Eatonton also is known for the Rock Eagle Effigy, a prehistoric rock effigy of a giant eagle believed to have been created by the Creek Indians about 5,000 years ago.

Another famous writer—one of the most famous in America—lived and worked in nearby Milledgeville. Flannery O'Connor's home at Andalusia Farm is open for tours. A collection of memorabilia is displayed at the Flannery O'Connor Memorial in the Ina D. Russell Library on the campus of Georgia College and State University. One of the early capitals of Georgia, Milledgeville is the site of the Old Governor's Mansion, a restored 1850s building, and the

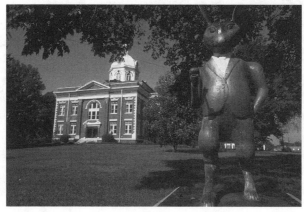

Br'er Rabbit at the courthouse square in Eatonton
GEORGIA DEPARTMENT OF ECONOMIC DEVELOPMENT

Old State Capitol Building, which houses exhibits on local history.

The small community of Juliette, located a few miles off I-75, is well worth a detour if you are a fan of the movie *Fried Green Tomatoes*. You can sample the fried delicacy at the Whistle Stop Café, tour the town, and visit the Old Mill Motorcycle Museum to see displays of vintage cycles. You can also tour the museum, farmhouse, gristmill, and cotton gin at the Jarrell Plantation Historic Site.

Macon, located an hour-and-a-half drive from Atlanta on I-75, is the music capital of the state. This is the city that produced Little Richard, Otis Redding, Capricorn Records, and the Allman Brothers Band, among others. The Georgia Music Hall of Fame celebrates all of Georgia's musical talent, including Ray Charles, Brenda Lee, R.E.M., Bill Anderson, and Ronnie Milsap. Macon is more than just music. Two highlights of the year are the Cherry Blossom Festival, when 270,000 cherry trees burst into bloom, and the nightly Lights on Macon tour, when thousands of lights illuminate some of the city's historic landmarks.

Here are some other places of interest in the heartland.

Blue Willow Inn and Village   Located in Social Circle, this restaurant in a 1907 Greek Revival mansion specializes in Southern food. A gift shop

The Georgia Music Hall of Fame
GEORGIA DEPARTMENT OF ECONOMIC DEVELOPMENT

Great Temple Mound at Ocmulgee National Monument

adjoining the restaurant sells Blue Willow china, among other things. The house was built by John Upshaw, uncle of Margaret Mitchell's first husband, Red Upshaw. Some *GWTW* fans surmised that Red Upshaw was the model for Rhett Butler, but Mitchell remained mum on the subject.

Cannonball House and Civil War Museum   Although Macon suffered little damage during the Civil War, local history buffs are particularly proud of the Cannonball House. Union troops apparently were aiming for the Hay House, an elegant Renaissance Revival mansion built in the 1850s, and hit the house two doors down by mistake. The cannonball itself is still on display.

Charlie Elliott Wildlife Center   This 6,400-acre preserve in Mansfield offers hiking, birding, hunting, and camping. Anglers can try their luck in one of the 29 ponds.

Georgia Sports Hall of Fame   Opened in 1999 in Macon, this building was designed to resemble a turn-of-the-20th-century ballpark with a green roof and a red-brick exterior. Inside are exhibits honoring more than 300 members, including Hank Aaron, Bobby Jones, and Ty Cobb.

Ocmulgee National Monument   This is where a civilization of Native Americans known as the Mississippians lived and died from 900 A.D. to 1100 A.D. The site on the Emery Highway near Macon includes the 45-foot Great Temple Mound, walking trails, and an archaeological museum.

Rose Hill Cemetery   This resting place of more than 600 Civil War soldiers is also where Duane Allman and Berry Oakley of the Allman Brothers Band are buried side by side in graves outlined in the shape of electric guitars.

Sidney Lanier Cottage   This is the birthplace of Georgia's most famous poet, Sidney Clopton Lanier. Lanier's best-known poems are "The Marshes of Glynn" and "Song of the Chattahoochee."

Altamaha River
GEORGIA DEPARTMENT OF ECONOMIC DEVELOPMENT

Magnolia Midlands

This south-central region of Georgia does indeed have an abundance of magnolias, but it also boasts four state parks, 20 public golf courses, lakes, rivers, lush farmland, and enough intriguing backroads to satisfy the most adventurous travelers. And don't forget all the farm produce and Vidalia onions. Even if you don't like onions—and a few odd people don't—you'll probably change your mind after tasting this sweet vegetable grown only in this part of the state. To learn more about these onions, or to sample onion products, take a tour of the UGA Vidalia Onion and Vegetable Research Center or Vidalia Onion Factory and Gifts. Both are in Vidalia, of course.

The midlands are a haven for fishermen, kayakers, and nature lovers. The Altamaha River, which ends on the coast, is formed where the Oconee, Ohoopee, and Ocmulgee rivers converge. The Nature Conservancy has listed the Altamaha as one of the "75 Last Great Places" because of the diversity of wildlife and native plants on its banks. And visitors to Moody Forest Natural Area in Baxley, with its forests of 300-year-old longleaf pines and 600-year-old tupelo cypress trees, can see what this part of Georgia looked like when the first settlers arrived.

Like the rest of the state, this region is steeped in history. Irwinville, home of Jefferson Davis Memorial State Historic Site, is famous as the location where the president of the Confederacy was captured in 1865.

Here are a few other places and attractions to consider.

Dublin   This picturesque town about 45 miles south of Macon off I-16 was founded by Irish settlers in 1812. That's why it goes all out for St. Patrick's Day every year. Dublin is also the home of another celebration that may or may not be something that makes citizens proud. Every summer, East Dublin is the site of the Redneck Games, a tongue-in-cheek festival featuring seed spitting, big-hair contests, cigarette flipping, hubcap hurling, and mud-pit belly flops.

Fruits and Nuts   You can get your Christmas dessert any time of the year in Claxton, "the Fruitcake Capital of the World." Tours (and samples) are available at the Claxton Bakery and the Georgia Fruit Cake Company. Visit the Pecan Orchard Plantation in Mount Vernon for pecans, a petting zoo, and an up-close look at a working farm. Strawberries, blackberries, peaches, and other pick-your-own fruits are available seasonally at Tom Sawyer Farms in Roddy. Clark Farm and Produce sells strawberries and pumpkins in season, along with homemade ice cream. In Reidsville, check with Farm Fresh Tattnall on South Main Street for directions to pick-your-own farms in the county. And in Dublin, be sure to visit the Market on Madison, where local farmers bring their produce to sell.

Guido Gardens   If you're looking for a quiet place to meditate, stop at these gardens in Metter. Named for syndicated radio evangelist Michael Guido, the gardens feature a prayer chapel, fountains, waterfalls, and inspirational music.

Statesboro   The home of Georgia Southern University offers several fascinating attractions. The Center of Wildlife Education and the Lamar Q. Ball Jr. Raptor Center present demonstrations featuring birds of prey and programs about reptiles. At the Georgia Southern University Museum, you can view prehistoric remains, including a 26-foot fossil of a mosasaur.

Carter Country

This southwestern part of the state is a prime peanut-farming area. It's also home to the world's most famous peanut farmer, former president Jimmy Carter. Carter's hometown of Plains is still a favorite stop for tourists, as is the Little White House in Warm Springs, where President Franklin D. Roosevelt stayed on trips to treat his legs in the warm mineral springs.

Former President Jimmy Carter
GEORGIA DEPARTMENT OF ECONOMIC DEVELOPMENT

Nearby Americus is the birthplace and headquarters of Habitat for Humanity. The idea for the volunteer organization began at Koinonia Farms, a utopian community that also started the Prison and Jail Project. Founded in 1942, Koinonia Farms still grows pecans, peanuts, and blueberries.

Columbus is the largest city in the area and the third-largest in the state. Founded as a frontier town on the Alabama border in 1827, Columbus supplied cannons and ironclad ships for the Confederacy. The city still retains much of its Old South charm while building for the future. A good example is the South Commons. Formerly a city dump and hospital for highly contagious patients, it is now a public green space and the site of the restored Memorial Stadium, the Columbus Civic Center, and Golden Park, where minor league baseball games are played.

Columbus is the home of Fort Benning, the largest infantry training facility in the world, and the birthplace of Carson McCullers, author of *The Heart Is a Lonely Hunter.* The city has a vibrant arts scene that includes museums, galleries, the Columbus Symphony Orchestra, and the historic Springer Opera House.

Here are some other places to visit in the area.

Andersonville National Historic Site A national cemetery, the National Prisoner of War Museum, and the remains of a stockade from a Civil War prison camp are stark reminders of the horrors of war. Nearly 13,000 Union prisoners held in Andersonville died from disease or starvation.

Callaway Gardens   Located in Pine Mountain, this private resort is set amid 2,500 acres of forests and flower gardens with hiking and biking trails, a 65-acre lake, golf courses, the Cecil B. Day Butterfly Center, and the John A. Sibley Horticultural Center. During summer, acrobats from the Florida State University circus perform regularly.

Fort Benning   The list of army legends who have served at the Infantry School of Arms here includes Generals George Patton and Dwight Eisenhower. The National Infantry Museum, located on the base, offers a collection of historic weapons and a re-created World War I barracks.

Ma Rainey House   This house at 805 Fifth Avenue in Columbus was the last home of Gertrude Pridgett "Ma" Rainey, a famous gospel and blues singer in the 1920s.

Pasaquan   This unusual art site in Buena Vista was created by Eddie Owens Martin, a sharecropper's son who changed his name to St. EOM when he became a folk artist. The exhibits include sculptures, colorful paintings, and totems from other cultures.

Springer Opera House   Located in Columbus, this was considered one of the finest entertainment venues in the Southeast in the days when performers such as Will Rogers entertained packed houses. After a period of deterioration, the theater was saved from demolition and restored to its former glory by a group of concerned citizens in the 1960s. The Springer is now the official State Theater of Georgia.

Westville   Located just outside Lumpkin, Westville is a re-creation of an 1850s town. The first house from that period was moved here in the late 1960s. Now, the town has 33 buildings, including a courthouse and a shoemaker's shop. Craftspeople perform their tasks dressed in authentic costumes.

Butterfly Center at Callaway Gardens
GEORGIA DEPARTMENT OF ECONOMIC DEVELOPMENT

Habitat for Humanity International

Volunteers work on a Habitat House.
HABITAT FOR HUMANITY INTERNATIONAL

Most Americans are familiar with Habitat for Humanity and its mission of building homes for people who could not otherwise afford them. Through volunteer labor and donations of money and materials, Habitat builds and rehabilitates simple, decent houses with the help of the homeowner (partner) families. Habitat houses are financed with affordable loans and sold to partner families at no profit. The homeowners' monthly mortgage payments are used to build still more Habitat houses. To date, Habitat volunteers have built or rehabilitated nearly 300,000 houses worldwide.

Habitat has dual headquarters in Americus and Atlanta. The organization was founded by Millard and Linda Fuller after the couple had become part of Koinonia, an interracial Christian community. The Fullers and Koinonia's founder, Clarence Jordan, developed a plan according to which volunteers would work with those in need to build affordable housing.

After building houses for thousands of Americans, Habitat expanded to other countries in 1973. The hands-on involvement of former president Jimmy Carter and his wife, Rosalynn, increased the visibility of Habitat for Humanity and sparked an increase in affiliates.

But reading about the success of Habitat for Humanity is not nearly as inspiring as seeing the results. At the Global Village and Discovery Center in Americus, visitors can tour a village of poverty housing and compare it with full-sized models of the types of houses Habitat has built in more than 15 countries, including Guatemala, Ghana, and Papua New Guinea.

Located at 721 West Church Street in Americus, the Global Village and Discovery Center is open Monday through Friday from 9 A.M. to 5 P.M. and Saturday from 10 A.M. to 2 P.M. from March through November. For information on the center, call 800-HABITAT, extension 7937, or visit www.habitat.org/gvdc. For information about Habitat for Humanity, visit www.habitat.org.

Agrirama wagon ride
GEORGIA DEPARTMENT OF
ECONOMIC DEVELOPMENT

Plantation Trace

This region is a land of pecan orchards, cotton fields, and pine forests. Once the home of ancient tribes of Native Americans, the land eventually was taken over by white settlers who came to carve out small farms. They were followed by timber barons and plantation owners who built elegant white-columned mansions.

The area was invaded again in the late 19th century when wealthy Northerners fled the bitter winters above the Mason-Dixon line. Resort hotels opened, and thousands of acres were transformed into quail- and fox-hunting retreats for the elite.

Here are the region's sightseeing highlights.

Albany   You'll give native Georgians a sure sign that you're not from around here if you mispronounce the name of this city about 190 miles south of Atlanta. It's al-BENNY, not ALL-bany. Located on the Flint River, Albany is "the Quail Capital of the World." More than 40 former cotton plantations have been converted to hunting preserves. Points of interest in Albany include the Albany Civil Rights Institute; the FlintRiverQuarium, a freshwater aquarium; and the Parks at Chehaw, where you'll find a wild animal park and a hiking trail.

Georgia Agrirama   Visitors can see what life was like on a working farm in the 1800s. Costumed guides conduct tours of two farmsteads and other exhibits at this living-history museum in Tifton.

Thomasville   Home of author Bailey White, this picturesque town attracted droves of Northern millionaires in the late 1800s after a medical article touted the health benefits of the pine-scented air. Many of the hunting plantations established then are still in business. Plantation houses open for tours include Pebble Hill Plantation, an 1820s Greek Revival mansion furnished with antiques and 33 original Audubon prints, and the Lapham-Patterson House, an 1884 Victorian mansion. Thomasville also is a city of roses. The Rose Test Gardens on U.S. 84 showcase 500 varieties of roses around a gazebo. Visitors can learn about local history at the Thomas County Historical Museum, which features vintage cars and a Victorian bowling alley.

Valdosta   Located 230 miles south of Atlanta, Valdosta is the home of Valdosta State University. It's also known as "the Azalea City" because of its many flowering gardens. Three National Register Historic Districts are located in town—the downtown, Patterson Street, and Victorian Fairview. For something to entertain the kids, go to Wild Adventures, a theme park with a safari train ride, water rides, and exotic animals.

State Parks

The following is a list of Georgia's state parks. For more details, visit www. gastateparks.org.

North Georgia

A. H. Stephens Historic Park   456 Alexander Street North, Crawfordville, Ga. 30631 (706-456-2602). Here, you can visit a Confederate museum and a restored 1875 house. The park offers cottages, hiking and equestrian trails, boating, fishing, and swimming. The museum is open Tuesday through Sunday, and the park is open daily. Call for hours and fees.

Amicalola Falls State Park and Lodge   418 Amicalola Falls Road, Dawsonville, Ga. 30534 (706-265-8888). Visitors enjoy the 729-foot waterfall, as well as hiking and camping. Cottages are available. The lodge offers rooms and a restaurant. The park is open daily from 7 A.M. to 10 P.M. A parking fee is charged; call for other fees.

Black Rock Mountain State Park   3085 Black Rock Mountain Parkway, Mountain City, Ga. 30562 (706-746-2141). People come here to hike the trails in Georgia's highest state park. Camping, fishing, and cottages are available. The park is open daily from 7 A.M. to 10 P.M. A parking fee is charged; call for other fees.

Bobby Brown State Park   2509 Bobby Brown State Park Road, Elberton,

Ga. 30635 (706-213-2046). Located on Clarks Hill Lake, the park offers boat rentals, swimming, fishing, hiking, and camping. It is open daily from 7 A.M. to 10 P.M. A parking fee is charged; call for other fees.

Cloudland Canyon State Park   122 Cloudland Canyon Road, Rising Fawn, Ga. 30738 (800-864-7275 or 706-657-4050). Located near Lookout Mountain and Rock City, the park offers scenic views of the canyon and waterfalls, trails for experienced hikers, cottages, camping, and tennis. A parking fee is charged; call for other fees.

Elijah Clark State Park   2959 McCormick Highway, Lincolnton, Ga. 30817 (800-864-7275 or 706-359-3458). Named after a Revolutionary War hero, this park offers swimming in Clarks Hill Lake, a beach, boating, mini-golf, camping, hiking, and a museum in a replica of Clark's cabin. It is open daily from 7 A.M. to 10 P.M. A parking fee is charged except on Wednesdays.

Fort Mountain State Park   181 Fort Mountain Road, Chatsworth, Ga. 30705 (800-864-7275 or 706-422-1932). The park offers an 855-foot rock wall at the top of the mountain, hiking trails, cottages, camping, horseback riding, and boat rentals. A parking fee is charged.

Fort Yargo State Park   210 South Broad Street, Winder, Ga. 30680 (770-867-3489). Located about 50 miles east of Atlanta, this park has boat rentals, a swimming area, mini-golf, picnicking facilities, and hiking trails. It is open daily from 7 A.M. to 10 P.M. A parking fee is charged; call for other fees.

Hard Labor Creek State Park   2438 Knox Chapel Road, Rutledge, Ga. 30663 (800-864-7275 or 706-557-3001). Amenities here include a golf course,

Hiking at Cloudland Canyon State Park
GEORGIA DEPARTMENT OF ECONOMIC DEVELOPMENT

hiking and horse trails, cottages, and campsites. The park is open daily from 7 A.M. to 10 P.M. A parking fee is charged.

Hart State Park   330 Hart State Park Road, Hartwell, Ga. 30643 (800-864-7275 or 706-376-8756). Located on Hartwell Lake, Hart State Park offers fishing, swimming, camping, cottages, and canoe rentals. It is open daily from 7 A.M. to 10 P.M. A parking fee is charged; call for other fees.

James H. Floyd State Park   U.S. 27 approximately three miles south of Summerville, Ga. (800-864-7275 or 706-857-0826). Fishermen (and fisherwomen) can try their luck in two stocked lakes in this quiet park. Hiking, camping, and cottages are also offered. The park is open daily from 7 A.M. to 10 P.M. A parking fee is charged; call for other fees.

John Tanner State Park   354 Tanners Beach Road, Carrollton, Ga. 30117 (800-864-7275 or 770-830-2222). This park offers boat rentals, motor lodge rooms, hiking, camping, and mini-golf. It is open daily from 7 A.M. to 10 P.M. A parking fee is charged; call for other fees.

Mistletoe State Park   3723 Mistletoe Road, Appling, Ga. 30802 (800-864-7275 or 706-541-0321). Located on Clarks Hill Lake, this park offers a beach, campsites, lodging, boat rentals, and biking and hiking trails. It is open daily from 7 A.M. to 10 P.M. A parking fee is charged.

Moccasin Creek State Park   3655 Ga. 197 North, Clarkesville, Ga. 30523 (800-864-7275 or 706-947-3194). Canoe rentals, a boat ramp, and a wheelchair-accessible fishing pier are some of the amenities at this park on Lake Burton. It is open daily from 7 A.M. to 10 P.M. A parking fee is charged; call for other fees.

Panola Mountain State Conservation Park   Ga. 155, Stockbridge, Ga. 30281 (800-864-7275 or 770-389-7801). Located 18 miles southeast of Atlanta, this mountain park features exhibits, rare plants, trails, and guided hikes. It is open daily from 7 A.M. until dusk. A parking fee is charged.

Red Top Mountain State Park and Lodge   Exit 285 off I-75 at Cartersville, Ga. 30121 (800-864-7275 or 770-975-4226). Located on Lake Allatoona, this park has a lodge, a restaurant, a beach, mini-golf, camping, and cottages. It is open daily from 7 A.M. to 10 P.M. A parking fee is charged; call for other fees.

Sweetwater Creek State Conservation Park   Mount Vernon Road, Lithia Springs, Ga. 30057 (800-864-7275 or 770-732-5871). This park offers fishing and boat rentals on its 215-acre lake, picnic shelters, playgrounds, and hiking trails to the ruins of a Civil War textile mill. It is open daily from 7 A.M. to 10 P.M. A parking fee is charged.

Tallulah Gorge State Park   338 Jane Hurt Yarn Drive, Tallulah Falls, Ga. 30573 (706-754-7970 or 770-754-7979 for camping information). Hiking trails and a suspension bridge allow breathtaking views of the gorge. The park also offers fishing, camping, and a gift shop. It is open daily from 8 A.M. until dark. A parking fee is charged.

Unicoi State Park and Lodge   1788 Ga. 356, Helen, Ga. 30545 (800-864-7275 or 706-878-2201). This park offers rooms at the lodge, a restaurant, cottages, camping, hiking, and boat rentals. It is open daily from 7 A.M. to 10 P.M. A parking fee is charged; call for other fees.

Victoria Bryant State Park and Golf Course   1105 Bryant Park Road, Royston, Ga. 30662 (706-245-6270). In addition to a golf course and pro shop, the park has a campground, a swimming pool, a playground, and picnic areas along a stream. It is open daily from 7 A.M. until dark. A parking fee is charged.

Vogel State Park   7485 Vogel State Park Road, Blairsville, Ga. 30512 (800-864-7275 or 706-745-2628). This park offers a lake with a beach, cottages, camping, mini-golf, and a Civilian Conservation Corps museum. It is open daily from 7 A.M. to 10 P.M. A parking fee is charged.

Watson Mill Bridge State Park   650 Watson Mill Road, Comer, Ga. 30629 (800-864-7275 or 706-783-5349). The covered bridge in this park dates to 1885 and is the longest in Georgia. Camping, hiking, and fishing are available. The park is open daily from 7 A.M. to 10 P.M. A parking fee is charged; call for other fees.

Southwestern Georgia

F. D. Roosevelt State Park   2970 Ga. 190, Pine Mountain, Ga. 31822 (800-864-7275 or 706-663-4858). This was one of President Roosevelt's favorite picnic sites. Amenities include camping, boat rentals, and horseback riding. The park is open daily from 7 A.M. to 10 P.M. A parking fee is charged.

Florence Marina State Park   Ga. 39-C, Lumpkin, Ga. 31815 (800-864-7275 or 229-838-4244). Located 16 miles west of Lumpkin, this park offers a fishing pier, a marina, boat rentals, cottages, camping, and a swimming pool. It is open daily from 7 A.M. to 10 P.M. A parking fee is charged; call for other fees.

George T. Bagby State Park and Lodge   Ga. 39, Fort Gaines, Ga. 39851 (800-864-7275 or 229-768-2571). This resort park four miles north of Fort Gaines offers a golf course, a marina, a lodge, boat rentals, cottages, and hiking. It is open daily from 7 A.M. to 10 P.M. A parking fee is charged; call for other fees.

Georgia Veterans Memorial State Park   2459-A U.S. 280 West, Cordele, Ga. 31015 (800-864-7275 or 229-276-2371). Situated on an 8,600-

F. D. Roosevelt State Park

acre lake, this park offers a military museum, cottages, camping, boating, and fishing. It is open daily from 7 A.M. to 10 P.M. A parking fee is charged; call for other fees.

High Falls State Park   76 High Falls Park Drive, Jackson, Ga. 30233 (800-864-7275 or 478-993-3053). Visitors to this park on the Towaliga River can hike to the ruins of an 1880s gristmill, rent boats, camp, and swim in the pool. The park is open daily from 7 A.M. to 10 P.M. A parking fee is charged.

Indian Springs State Park   678 Lake Clark Road, Indian Springs, Ga. 30216 (800-864-7275 or 770-504-2277). Indians and travelers believed that the springs here had healing powers. The property was acquired by the state in 1825 and became a state forest park in 1927. Visitors can sample the spring water, tour the historic buildings, swim, boat, and hike. The park is open daily from 7 A.M. to 10 P.M. A parking fee is charged.

Kolomoki Mounds State Historic Park   U.S. 27, Blakely, Ga. 39823 (800-864-7275 or 229-724-2150). Located six miles north of Blakely, these seven Native American mounds date to between 250 A.D. and 950 A.D. The park offers a museum and boat rentals. It is open daily from 8 A.M. to 5 P.M. A parking fee is charged; call for other fees.

Providence Canyon State Park   Ga. 89-C, Lumpkin, Ga. 31815 (800-864-7275 or 229-838-6202). Located seven miles west of Lumpkin, Georgia's "Little Grand Canyon" offers spectacular views and hiking trails. A parking fee is charged; call for hours and other fees. (See photograph on page 14).

Reed Bingham State Park   Exit 39 off I-75 onto Ga. 37, Adel, Ga. 31620 (800-864-7275 or 229-896-3551). This park is six miles west of Adel.

Located on a 375-acre lake, it offers fishing, watersports, boat tours, mini-golf, camping, and picnicking. The park is open daily from 7 A.M. to 10 P.M. A parking fee is charged.

Seminole State Park   7870 State Park Drive, Donaldsonville, Ga. 39845 (229-861-3137). Visitors can rent canoes and go bird watching, camping, swimming, and hiking.

Sprewell Bluff State Park   740 Sprewell Bluff Road, Thomaston, Ga. 30286 (800-864-7275 or 706-646-6026). Visitors can hike along the Flint River, go picnicking, and enjoy horseshoes and volleyball. The park is open daily from 7 A.M. until dark. A parking fee is charged.

Coastal Georgia

Crooked River State Park   6222 Charlie Smith Sr. Highway, St. Marys, Ga. 31558 (800-864-7275 or 912-882-5256). This park was the site of the McIntosh Sugar Works, built in 1825 and used as a starch factory during the Civil War. Today, it offers a boat ramp, mini-golf, cottages, campsites, and fishing. Visitors can rent kayaks from a nearby outfitter. Ferry trips to Cumberland Island are available.

General Coffee State Park   Ga. 32, Nicholls, Ga. 31544 (800-864-7275 or 912-384-7082). Located six miles east of Douglas, this park has farm buildings, animals, cottages, a 19th-century house for rent, boat rentals, camping, fishing, and a swimming pool.

George L. Smith State Park   371 George L. Smith Park Road, Twin City, Ga. 30471 (800-864-7275 or 478-763-2759). Named for a former Georgia legislator, this park includes such attractions as a covered bridge, a gristmill, and a millpond that is a favorite spot for bird watchers. It offers camping, fishing, cottages, and boat rentals. The park is open daily from 7 A.M. to 10 P.M. A parking fee is charged.

Gordonia-Altamaha State Park   U.S. 280, Reidsville, Ga. 30453 (800-864-7275 or 912-557-7744). Amenities at this park include a golf course, a pro shop, tennis courts, mini-golf, boat rentals, and camping and picnic areas. The park is open daily from 7 A.M. to 10 P.M. A parking fee is charged.

Hamburg State Park   6071 Hamburg State Park Road, Mitchell, Ga. 30802 (800-864-7275 or 478-552-2393). This park on a 225-acre lake offers a museum, a restored gristmill, a 1920s country store, boat rentals, fishing, and hiking. It is open daily from 7 A.M. to 10 P.M. A parking fee is charged.

Laura S. Walker State Park   5653 Laura Walker Road, Waycross, Ga. 31503 (800-864-7275 or 912-287-4900). Located near the Okefenokee Swamp, this park was named for a Georgia writer and naturalist. Its nature trails showcase a variety of wildlife, including alligators, owls, and blue herons. Other attractions include an 18-hole golf course, a pro shop, boat rentals, fishing, a swimming pool, and picnic areas. The park is open daily from 7 A.M. to 10 P.M. A parking fee is charged.

Little Ocmulgee State Park and Lodge   U.S. 441, McRae, Ga. 31055 (877-591-5572 or 229-868-7474). Located two miles north of McRae on a 265-acre lake, this park has a golf course, a lodge, a restaurant, a nature trail, and a visitor center. It is open daily from 7 A.M. to 10 P.M.; the lodge is open 24 hours a day. A parking fee is charged.

Magnolia Springs State Park   1053 Magnolia Springs Drive, Millen, Ga. 30442 (800-864-7275 or 478-982-1660). Famous for its crystal-clear springs, the park site was a prison called Camp Lawton during the Civil War. Today, the park has a freshwater aquarium, a boardwalk, cottages, boat rentals, and hiking trails. It is open daily from 7 A.M. to 10 P.M. A parking fee is charged.

Stephen C. Foster State Park   17515 Ga. 177, Fargo, Ga. 31631 (800-864-7275 or 912-637-5274). Located on the banks of the Suwannee River, this park is aptly named for the famous songwriter. It also is the gateway to the Okefenokee National Wildlife Refuge. A parking fee is charged; call for hours and other fees.

Hunting and Fishing Licenses

Anyone 16 or older is required to have a current Georgia fishing license in his or her possession while fishing in fresh water or salt water in Georgia. Identification may be required by Georgia conservation rangers. Exceptions are made for fishing in privately owned ponds and for landowners and their immediate families fishing on their own land.

Proof of residence (a Georgia driver's license or other ID) is required to purchase a fishing license. Resident anglers from 16 to 64 are required to have a current Georgia fishing license in their possession while fishing. Residents 65 or older may fish with a Senior Lifetime License. Residents who are permanently and totally disabled may obtain a Disability Honorary Combination Hunting and Fishing License by providing proof of their disability. Blind residents must provide a physician's certification of blindness with the application.

Nonresidents under 16 do not need a fishing or trout license. Those 16 or older must have a current nonresident Georgia fishing license to fish in Georgia, except in private ponds. College students enrolled full time in

Georgia may purchase a resident fishing license if they have a current student ID. Military personnel on active status at a Georgia base and their immediate family members may buy a resident fishing license.

All residents between the ages of 16 and 64 must have a trout license as well as a current fishing license to fish in designated trout waters. Residents with a Senior Lifetime License and honorary license holders are not required to have a trout license. Nonresident anglers must have a nonresident fishing license and a trout license to fish in designated trout waters.

All recreational hunting and fishing licenses are good for one year from the date of purchase.

A regular fishing license for residents is $9. A nonresident license is $24 for a season, $7 for seven days, or $3.50 for one day. A trout license is $5 for a resident and $13 for a nonresident. A combination fishing and hunting license is $17 for a resident; it is not available for nonresidents. A license for wildlife management areas is $19 for residents and $73 for nonresidents.

A sportsman's license includes fishing, trout fishing, wildlife management area, hunting, big-game hunting, primitive weapons hunting, and waterfowl conservation licenses. It can be purchased for $60. It does not include the federal duck stamp. Sportsman's licenses are not available for nonresidents.

Lifetime hunting and fishing licenses are available for the following fees: $200 for infants under age two; $350 for children between two and 15; and $500 for adults 16 and older. A Senior Discount Lifetime License costs $95; seniors 65 and older can obtain a free Honorary Lifetime License. You must be a Georgia resident for at least 12 months immediately prior to applying for a lifetime license. The license is valid even if you move out of state. Lifetime licenses for nonresident grandchildren ages 15 and younger are available for $1,000.

Georgia fishing licenses are available at more than 1,100 discount stores, marinas, and stores that sell sporting goods, bait and tackle, and hardware. Licenses can also be purchased in person at the Department of Natural Resources, License Unit, 2065 U.S. 178, Social Circle, Ga. 30025 (800-366-2661). Your Social Security number is required at the time of purchase.

Boating Rules and Fees

Owners must obtain a certificate and a decal before operating their boats in Georgia. Boat registration applications are available from any Wildlife Resources Division office and from boat dealers, hardware and sporting goods

Boating on Lake Oconee
GEORGIA DEPARTMENT OF ECONOMIC DEVELOPMENT

stores, and marinas. The temporary certificate on the registration form allows owners to operate their boats until they receive a permanent certificate and decal by mail.

Fees for a three-year boat registration are as follows: $15 for boats less than 16 feet (class A); $36 for boats 16 to 26 feet (class 1); $90 for boats 26 to 40 feet (class 2); and $150 for boats 40 feet or longer (class 3). Additional fees include $3 for transfer, $1 for duplicates, and $5 for marine toilets.

Boats must have a life jacket for each person aboard, as well as a throwable floatation device. Boats may be operated only by persons 16 or older. They may not be operated faster than idling speed within 100 feet of other boats, people, or the shoreline near beaches, residences, and public-use areas. A five-miles-per-hour speed limit is in force for Jet Skis in those same areas.

Festivals

Food festivals are listed at the end of the "Food and Drink" chapter. Here is a list of other festivals:

Crape Myrtle Festival, Marshallville (July)
Redneck Games, East Dublin (July)
Georgia Mountain Fair, Hiawassee (July)
Annual Butternut Creek Festival, Blairsville (July)
Winged Wonders Butterfly Festival, Thomasville (July)

Bluegrass Festival
GEORGIA DEPARTMENT OF ECONOMIC DEVELOPMENT

Commerce Crossing Art & Antique Fest, Commerce (August)
Pigs and Peaches BBQ Cookoff, Kennesaw (August)
Angel City Bluegrass Festival, Unadilla (August)
Grant Park Summer Shade Festival, Atlanta (August)
Decatur Book Festival, Decatur (Labor Day weekend)
Mountain Marketplace Heritage Festival, Blairsville (Labor Day weekend)
Farm Day Festival, Lumber City (September)
Lovejoy Autumn Festival, Lovejoy (September)
North Georgia State Fair, Marietta (September)
Annual Fall Bluegrass Festival, Cochran (September)
Westobou Festival, Augusta (September)
Sandy Springs Festival, Sandy Springs (September)
Family Fun Day, Bogart (September)
Union Junction Jamboree, Union Point (September)
La Fiesta del Pueblo, Tifton (September)
Shady Days in Gay, Gay (October)
Friendship Festival, Social Circle (October)
Cotton Pickin' Fair, Gay (October)
Sherman's Last Burning Fall Festival, Covington (October)
Sorghum Festival, Blairsville (October)
Cochran-Bleckley Country Fest, Cochran (October)
Hummingbird Festival, Hogansville (October)

Books and Resources

Atlanta Travel Guide. www.atlanta.net.

Explore Georgia. www.explorega.org.

Georgia Travel Guide. www.georgia.org.

Homan, Tim. *Hiking Trails of North Georgia*. Atlanta, Ga.: Peachtree Publishers, 1997.

Lenz, Richard J. *Highroad Guide to the Georgia Coast and Okefenokee*. Winston-Salem, N.C.: John F. Blair, Publisher, 2003.

Northeast Georgia Travel Association. www.georgiamountains.org.

Porter, Darwin, and Danford Prince. *Frommer's Portable Savannah*. Frommer's, 2005.

Food and Drink

New World of Coca-Cola features artifacts and multimedia exhibits tracing the history of the famous soft drink.
COURTESY OF NEW WORLD OF COCA-COLA

It's not true that all Georgians drink Coca-Cola for breakfast, but we do consume a lot of the bubbly beverage invented by Atlanta pharmacist John Pemberton in the late 19th century.

Coke is the biggest soft drink company in Georgia, but it's not the only one. Another famous beverage is RC (or Royal Crown) Cola, concocted in Columbus in 1905 by Claude A. Hatcher. RC became known as the beverage of choice when you're eating a MoonPie—a ubiquitous Southern snack that consists of two large cookies with a marshmallow filling. Hatcher's company introduced fruit-flavored soft drinks called Nehi in 1924.

Some die-hard Coca-Cola lovers still buy the drink in glass bottles. If you want to appear to be a longtime Georgian, take a pack of salted peanuts and pour it into the Coke bottle before you drink. Purists use only peanuts from Tom's, a Columbus company that specializes in peanuts, crackers, and other snack foods.

What else do Georgians eat? Well, grits, of course, preferably stone-ground and seasoned with salt, pepper, butter, or red-eye gravy made from country ham. Only Yankees or lazy Southerners eat instant grits, and no true Southerner puts sugar on them. In 2002, the Georgia legislature proclaimed grits the state's "official prepared food." Grits also are tasty cooked with shrimp (one of Georgia's most prized seafood crops) or served with fried catfish.

Georgians love barbecue, too, though we're not as fanatical about it as North Carolinians. Most of our barbecued pork is flavored with tomato-based sauces. To try a sample of the different kinds of barbecue, check out the Slosheye Trail Big Pig Jig. Held every fall in Vienna, this cookoff is considered one of the top barbecue contests in the country.

We are even fussier about Brunswick stew. Georgians have long engaged in a war of words with Virginians, who claim to have invented the delicacy and ignore the fact that it obviously was named after the Georgia city of Brunswick. Virginians prefer chicken as the main meat ingredient; Georgians like pork and beef. Recipes vary but usually include tomatoes, lima beans, corn, chicken, pork, and beef. Some folks substitute squirrel, rabbit, or venison, but whatever ingredients you throw in the pot, make sure the stew is thick and hearty. Otherwise, it's just soup.

Since Georgia is known as "the Peach State," it will come as no surprise that we consume peaches in great quantities. The same goes for peanuts, one of the state's major crops. If you've moved here from somewhere north or west of the Mason-Dixon line, you may be unfamiliar with boiled peanuts. Boiled peanuts are cooked in the shell in salted water until tender. Black iron pots of boiled peanuts are a common sight at roadside stands in the fall.

Visiting these roadside stands and some of the larger farmers' markets in Georgia is a good way to become acquainted with the variety of the state's produce. The Atlanta State Farmers Market in Forest Park south of the city is a hub of activity during spring, summer, and fall. Many farmers sell pick-your-own strawberries and other fruits in season. Kauffman's Farmarket in

Georgia is known as "the Peach State."
GEORGIA DEPARTMENT OF ECONOMIC DEVELOPMENT

Roadside stand
GEORGIA DEPARTMENT OF ECONOMIC DEVELOPMENT

Montezuma offers strawberries and other vegetables, and Taylor Orchards in Reynolds sells peaches and strawberries. Up in North Georgia near Alto, Jaemor Farms offers fresh seasonal fruits and vegetables, as well as pickles and preserves.

When the frost is on the pumpkin, you can find the traditional Halloween fruit at Burt's Farm in Dawsonville, Grandpa Jones Corn Maze and Pumpkins in Ellijay, any farmers' market, and most roadside stands. This is the season when the owners of apple orchards in North Georgia bring out their harvests, along with cider, jellies, and fried apple pies. Hillcrest Orchards and Panorama Orchards in Ellijay offer apples, sorghum syrup, and other delicacies for sale; they also feature seasonal self-picking. Mercier Orchards in Blue Ridge begins picking apples in September.

If you belong to that unique group that loves fruitcake, you can find

Burt's Farm in Dawsonville
GEORGIA DEPARTMENT OF ECONOMIC DEVELOPMENT

Georgia's official vegetable is the Vidalia onion.
GEORGIA DEPARTMENT OF ECONOMIC DEVELOPMENT

enough for the entire extended family at Claxton, "the Fruitcake Capital of the World." The Trappist monks at the Monastery of the Holy Spirit in Conyers also make fruitcakes, fudge, and other baked goods for sale.

Georgia's official vegetable is the Vidalia onion, a sweet onion first grown near Vidalia in the early 1930s. Vidalia onions are now protected by trademark. The name can be used to market onions grown only in a designated area in South Georgia.

Vidalia onions are delicious fried or chopped up with Hoppin' John, another favorite dish of Georgians and most Southerners. Hoppin' John is black-eyed peas and rice cooked with a chunk of ham, bacon, or hog jowl. Hoppin' John and collard greens are a traditional New Year's Day meal, said to bring good luck (and money) the rest of the year. Maybe it does for the farmers who sell the peas and collards. By the way, you can find peas for Hoppin' John, butterbeans (lima beans), tomatoes, and other vegetables at Calhoun Produce in Ashburn.

Georgia also produces dairy products and cheese. Sweet Grass Dairy in Thomasville and Flat Creek Lodge in Swainsboro are well known for their gourmet cheeses.

Tastes are different along the Georgia coast, where seafood and the Gullah cuisine are plentiful. The Gullahs, or Geechees, live on the barrier islands and are known for their unique seafood and rice dishes.

Fried chicken, fried pork chops, fried seafood, and fried green tomatoes are still regular items on many menus in Georgia, despite increased awareness of cholesterol problems and the emergence of "New South" chefs who serve

Boiled peanuts
GEORGIA DEPARTMENT OF ECONOMIC DEVELOPMENT

If you're going to be a true Georgian, you have to learn the proper way to eat peanuts. I know, you've probably been eating roasted peanuts at baseball games all your life. Well, we eat roasted peanuts in the shell in Georgia, but we also eat them unshelled and salted, and we especially eat boiled peanuts. Here are a few tips on the cooking and consumption of "goober peas."

First of all, we like salted peanuts in those little cellophane packets. Old-time Southerners rip the top off the packet and pour the salted peanuts into a bottle of Coca-Cola (the seven-ounce size) or Royal Crown Cola. Then they drink the beverage quickly, before the peanuts get soggy.

Misguided individuals may suggest dropping boiled peanuts into a bottle of Coke or RC. That may work for some, but it's just not what most people in Georgia do. Stick with roasted peanuts if you're going to dunk them in your favorite bottled beverage.

Boiled peanuts are the official snack food of South Carolina, but that doesn't keep Georgians (and tourists) from consuming great quantities of them. Boiled peanuts are prepared by taking a fresh crop of just-picked green peanuts (they aren't colored green, they're pink and moist) and dropping them unshelled into a pot of salted water. Usually about a cup of salt for every two pounds of peanuts is adequate. Add enough water to cover the peanuts completely. Cook them for at least an hour, maybe two, then check a couple of the peanuts to see if they're soft. If they're crunchy, cook them longer. If they aren't salty enough, let them sit in the salted water for several hours. A word of caution: don't use peanuts that are mature or dry. They won't be as tasty. And make sure you store boiled peanuts in the refrigerator or they'll get slimy overnight.

If this sounds like too much trouble, just wait until early fall and take a trip to the mountains or to peanut country in South Georgia. There, you'll find roadside stands with bubbling pots of boiled peanuts for sale. They may or may not taste as good as the ones you cook at home, but that's the price you pay for being lazy.

Southern cooking
GEORGIA DEPARTMENT OF ECONOMIC DEVELOPMENT

gourmet—and healthier—versions of traditional Southern dishes.

If one Georgian can be credited—or blamed—for popularizing Southern food, it's Paula Deen, the star of a cooking show on the Food Network. Deen, who began her culinary career by selling bag lunches in Savannah, now owns The Lady & Sons restaurant. She is the author of several best-selling cookbooks and even has her own magazine.

And let's not forget the chili dog. Famous Georgia humorist and syndicated columnist Lewis Grizzard offered a tribute to the delicacy in his book *Chili Dogs Always Bark at Night*. While some purists may argue that the hot dog is not really a traditional Southern food, it is clear to most Georgians that it is as Southern as grits and sausage gravy. I'm not talking about the Coney Island dog or the Chicago dog with sauerkraut and other condiments. I'm talking about the kind of chili dog you find in country stores, pool halls, and The Varsity.

Billed as "the World's Largest Drive-In," The Varsity in Atlanta was founded more than 75 years ago by Georgia Tech dropout Frank Gordy. The restaurant has curb-hops and sit-down dining and a menu of chili dogs, chili cheeseburgers, French fries, and fried onion rings, guaranteed to boost anyone's cholesterol. The Varsity has expanded from its original location next to the Georgia Tech campus to open restaurants in Gwinnett County, Cobb County, and Athens.

Home-Grown Food Companies

Taking to heart Scarlett O'Hara's postwar vow of never going hungry again, Georgians have launched a number of food companies to make sure they don't. Here is a little information about the companies that provide breakfasts, lunches, dinners, desserts, and bubbly refreshments.

The Coca-Cola Company   Atlanta and Coca-Cola go hand in hand like, well, Coca-Cola and salted peanuts. Not long after John Pemberton served the first glass of his new concoction at Jacobs' Pharmacy in 1876, Coca-Cola became a local and regional favorite. Robert W. Woodruff, who became president of the company in 1923, took Coke to international markets. At the beginning of World War II, he promised to provide a Coke for a nickel to every American serviceman. This patriotic gesture resulted in the building of bottling plants around the world and made Coca-Cola a symbol of America.

Royal Crown Cola Company   Royal Crown (RC) never overtook Coca-Cola's lead as the most popular soft drink in the world, but it did become a memorable part of Southern culture. Even today, some people insist on having an RC and a MoonPie at least once a week. There's even a famous country song called "RC Cola and Moon Pie." Based in Columbus, Royal Crown was the first in the soft-drink industry to introduce a diet cola, a caffeine-free diet cola, and aluminum cans. In 2000, the British company Cadbury Schweppes bought RC Cola.

Tom's Foods   What would a Coke or an RC be without salted peanuts or peanut butter and cheese crackers? A few decades after soft drinks became a daily treat for Georgians, the Tom Huston Peanut Company began selling individual packages of roasted peanuts. In 1926, John Thomas "Tom" Huston of Columbus trademarked the familiar package with its red triangular logo. The company changed hands several times and was bought by General Mills in 1966. In 1970, the company became Tom's Foods. Lance, Inc., bought the company in 2005. Tom's now makes pretzels, potato chips, cookies, pastries, and candy bars, but roasted peanuts are still its best seller.

Stuckey's If you've ever driven through Georgia on the way to or from Florida, chances are you've stopped at a Stuckey's. The company began when Williamson S. Stuckey, Sr., of Eastman set up a roadside stand on Ga. 23 to sell his pecans. Nut sales were so successful that he added his wife's homemade pecan candies. The Stuckey's Pecan Log Roll, made of roasted nuts, white molasses, and sugar, became its trademark product. As business increased, the company added a restaurant and souvenir shop. Today, Stuckey's has become a Southern roadside icon, boasting more than 200 stores in 19 states.

Chick-fil-A Since Chick-fil-A has restaurants in 38 states, you've probably enjoyed one of its chicken sandwiches. Now that you're in Georgia, you can see where it all began. Founder Truett Cathy started the business at the Dwarf Grill in Hapeville by developing a pressure-cooked, fried, boneless chicken breast sandwich. As the company grew, it expanded the menu to include grilled chicken sandwiches, chicken salad, and chicken wraps. A major reason for the company's growth, besides the delicious food, is a national marketing campaign using cows on billboards and in TV ads urging people to "Eat Mor Chikin." As a result, Chick-fil-A has reported sales of more than $1.75 billion annually and employs more than 46,000 people. It is the second-largest fast-food chicken restaurant in the country.

Waffle House The bright yellow signs of this restaurant chain are as familiar in Georgia—and the rest of the nation—as McDonald's golden arches. Among family-style eateries, only Denny's is larger than this restaurant that offers breakfasts (waffles and eggs, of course), T-bone steaks, sandwiches, and other items 24 hours a day, 365 days a year. DeKalb County neighbors Joe Rogers and Tom Forkner launched Waffle House in 1955. One of its specialties, besides waffles, is hash brown potatoes prepared in different ways—scattered (plain), smothered (with onions), or covered (with cheese). Or you can get them smothered and covered. Waffle House has become a Southern cultural icon. In 2000, the rock band Hootie and the Blowfish released a CD entitled, "Scattered, Smothered and Covered," with a picture of a Waffle House on the cover. Atlanta's Jeff Foxworthy and his fellow Blue Collar Comedy Tour comedians performed one of their skits while sitting in a Waffle House.

Huddle House Founded in DeKalb County in 1964 by John Sparks, Huddle House now has 400 restaurants in 14 states. Like its competitor Waffle House, Huddle House serves breakfasts and other meals 24 hours a day, 365 days a year. Menu items include butterfly shrimp, chicken wings, and sandwiches.

Food Festivals

The best way to become acquainted with Georgia food is to sample lots of it. And the best way to do that, other than eating at every mom-and-pop restaurant in the state, is to attend some of the following food festivals:

International Chili Society's Georgia State Cookoff, Rocco's Pub, Marietta (spring)
National Grits Festival, Warwick (spring)
Vidalia Onion Festival, Vidalia (spring)
Georgia Blueberry Festival, Alma (June)
Georgia Sea Island Festival, St. Simons Island (June)
Georgia Peach Festival, Peach County (June)
Watermelon Days Festival, Cordele (June)
Georgia Barbecue Classic, Cartersville (June)
Dillard Bluegrass & Barbecue Festival, Dillard (August)
BBQ, Blues & Bluegrass Festival, Decatur (August)
Tom Watson Watermelon Festival, Thomson (August)
Annual Labor Day Catfish Festival, Kingsland
Shrimp & Grits: The Wild Georgia Shrimp Festival, Jekyll Island (September)
The Great Miller Lite Chili Cookoff, Stone Mountain Park (September)
Apple Festival, Ellijay (October)
Cherokee Pignic, Canton (October)
Sorghum Festival, Blairsville (October)
Slosheye Trail Big Pig Jig, Vienna (fall)
Plains Peanut Festival, Plains (fall)
Savannah Seafood Festival, Savannah (November)
National BBQ Festival, Douglas (November)

Wineries

Newcomers may be surprised to learn that Georgia is part of the winery renaissance sweeping the country. In 1900, Georgia was ranked sixth among grape-growing states. That was before Prohibition laws put an end to winemaking; Georgia banned alcoholic beverages in 1907. Eight decades later, farm bills were passed allowing winemaking to resume. Now, wineries are located all over northeastern Georgia.

Château Elan in Braselton is probably the best known because of the impressive 16th-century-style French château that houses the winery, restaurants, and a gift shop. Adjoining the château is a four-star hotel with more restaurants and a spa.

The mountain town of Dahlonega is home to four wineries: Montaluce Winery and Vineyards, Frogtown Cellars, BlackStock Vineyards, and Wolf Mountain Vineyards. Other wineries include Persimmon Creek Vineyards in Clayton, Sharp Mountain Vineyard in Jasper, Tiger Mountain Vineyards in Tiger, Habersham Winery in Helen, and Crane Creek Vineyards in Young Harris.

For more information about the wineries and a calendar of tasting events, visit www.georgiawine.com, the website of the Winegrowers Association of Georgia.

BOOKS AND RESOURCES

Brown, Fred, and Sherri M. L. Smith. *The Best of Georgia Farms: A Cookbook and Tour Book*. CI Publishing, 1998.

Dabney, Joseph Earl. *Smokehouse Hams, Spoon Bread & Scuppernong Wine: The Folklore of Southern Appalachian Cooking*. Nashville, Tenn.: Cumberland House, 1998.

Edge, John T. *A Gracious Plenty: Recipes and Recollections from the American South*. New York: Putnam, 1999.

Lewis, Edna, and Scott Peacock. *The Gift of Southern Cooking*. New York: Knopf, 2003.

New Georgia Encyclopedia. www.georgiaencyclopedia.org.

Arts and Entertainment

Little Richard
GEORGIA DEPARTMENT OF ECONOMIC DEVELOPMENT

Newcomers to Georgia need not worry about entering a cultural wasteland. If you like fine art, you can find it at the many museums in the state, including the High Museum of Art in Atlanta, the Morris Museum in Augusta, and the Telfair Museum of Art in Savannah. If you like folk art and crafts, you came to the right place. Folk art by Howard Finster and pottery by the Meaders family may be admired or purchased, if you're willing to pay handsomely.

You'll hear music everywhere in the state, from blues to bluegrass, from Handel to hip-hop. To get an idea of Georgia's musical history, take a trip to Macon and browse the Georgia Music Hall of Fame, where you can hear the works of Ray Charles, James Brown, Blind Willie McTell, Johnny Mercer, and other native sons.

Theater is alive and well in Georgia, too. The Alliance Theatre in Atlanta is the largest regional theater in the Southeast, and Atlanta's restored Fox Theatre brings in touring Broadway plays.

Other cities have vibrant community theater and restored movie palaces that now host live performances. The 1921 Lucas Theatre in Savannah was saved from oblivion by community activists and reopened in 2000. The Historic Savannah Theatre has been transformed and refurbished as a venue for local and touring performances. Columbus is home to the famous Springer Opera House, a 137-year-old facility that is the official State Theater of Georgia. In 1964, it, too, was saved by community efforts and restored to its 1871 Edwardian glory. Also in Columbus is the Liberty Theatre, the city's first black theater when it opened in 1924. The Liberty has hosted Ella Fitzgerald, Lena Horne, and other renowned black performers. Listed on the National Register of Historic Places, it now hosts arts performances for all audiences.

Other historic theaters in Georgia that have avoided the wrecking ball are the 1921 Rylander in Americus, the 1920s Douglass Theatre and the 1884 Grand Opera House in Macon, the 1910 Morton Theatre in Athens, the 1916 Imperial Theatre in Augusta, the 1945 Holly Theatre in Dahlonega, the 1940 Historic Elbert Theatre in Elberton, the 1941 Wink Theatre in Dalton, the 1929 DeSoto Theatre in Rome, and the 1930 Grand Theatre in Cartersville.

Three must-see performances are *Swamp Gravy*, the state's official folklife play, which runs from July to October in Colquitt; *Heaven Bound*, an African-American folk drama, performed in Atlanta; and *Cotton Patch Gospel*, a musical translation of the New Testament, performed in various venues.

Traditional crafts such as weaving, woodcarving, and quilting are flourishing in Georgia. Visitors can see demonstrations at various craft fairs and at the Foxfire Museum and Heritage Center in Rabun County.

The literary scene in Georgia has undergone remarkable growth since Margaret Mitchell put Atlanta on the map with *Gone With the Wind*. New writers, both natives and newcomers, are adding to the legacy of Flannery O'Connor, Carson McCullers, and Erskine Caldwell. Each year, more than 50,000 people attend the *Atlanta Journal-Constitution* Decatur Book Festival to hear regional talent, as well as some of the nation's major authors.

The following is a sample of what Georgia has to offer in the way of arts and entertainment. You'll find much more to enjoy, depending on the part of the state where you live.

Atlanta Symphony
GEORGIA DEPARTMENT OF ECONOMIC DEVELOPMENT

Music

Georgia's music is as diverse as its population, and has been for nearly 200 years. Before the Civil War, Georgians basically had the same taste as other Americans. They attended classical music concerts, operas, and gospel singings. In rural Georgia, Sacred Harp, a form in which the singers' voices "shaped" the notes, was popular.

Today, you can find any type of live music in most of the larger cities. The Atlanta Symphony became one of the leading orchestras in the country after Robert Shaw was named director in 1967. Atlanta also has several music clubs for local and regional performers, from blues to rock. Atlanta's Chastain Park, an open-air arena featuring tables for candlelight dining, is a popular site for touring musical acts.

Country Music

Folk music had always been around, but it became overshadowed in 1927 by something called "country music" after Victor Records set up a recording studio in Bristol, Tennessee, and invited area musicians to come in. In addition to Jimmy Rodgers and the Carter Family, a Georgia cotton mill worker, Fiddlin' John Carson, made a recording. Carson's record became such a success that the company sought other performers in a similar style.

Georgia native Ray Charles is not known as a country artist, but his 1992 record, *Modern Sounds in Country and Western Music*, brought this type of music to a broader audience. Other nationally known singers from Georgia include Bill Anderson of Commerce, Brenda Lee of Lithonia, Ronnie Milsap of Young Harris, Travis Tritt of Marietta, Trisha Yearwood of Monticello, Ray Stevens of Clarksdale, Doug Stone and Alan Jackson of Newnan, and Jerry Reed of Atlanta. Reed was probably best known for his acting role as Burt Reynolds's sidekick in the *Smokey and the Bandit* movies.

Boudreaux Bryant of Moultrie and his wife, Felice, were one of the most successful songwriting teams in country music. Their hits included "Rocky Top" and several Everly Brothers songs.

Rhythm-and-Blues

Mississippians would argue otherwise, but Georgia can also claim to be the birthplace of the blues. An English visitor in 1839 first made reference to the rice-plantation slave songs and music that later would be called "the blues." Wherever the genre was born, Georgia is the home of some of the greatest blues artists.

Gertrude "Ma" Rainey of Columbus is said to have been the first to sing blues in vaudeville, around 1900. Also around that time, blues musicians Georgia Tom Dorsey of Villa Rica, Piano Red (William Perryman) of Hampton, and others performed in clubs in Atlanta. Blind Willie McTell of Thomson was a well-known blues singer who performed in Atlanta from the 1920s until the 1950s. He was often joined by Piano Red and Curley Weaver of Covington.

Beginning in the late 1950s, rhythm-and-blues artists such as Chuck Willis, Ray Charles, Little Richard, and James Brown became nationally known.

Willis—best known for the hit song "What Am I Living For?"—also composed songs for Buddy Holly and Elvis Presley.

Ray Charles of Albany was a recording star in several fields, including rhythm-and-blues, country, gospel, and pop. His first big hit, "I Got a Woman," was recorded in Atlanta. Anyone who has seen *Ray*, the film about Charles, knows that the musician overcame blindness, poverty, drug addiction, and racial discrimination to become an icon.

Little Richard (Richard Penniman) is an over-the-top showman from Macon. His 1950s songs such as "Long Tall Sally" and "Tutti-Frutti" became hits on the rock-'n'-roll charts.

Perhaps the most influential rhythm-and-blues singer was James Brown of Augusta. Proclaimed "the Godfather of Soul" and "the hardest-working man in show business," Brown was a dynamic stage performer whose biggest

Usher
Georgia Music Hall of Fame

hits included "Please, Please, Please," "Papa's Got a Brand New Bag," and "I Got You (I Feel Good)."

Another great R&B singer who crossed over to popular music was Otis Redding, born in 1941 in Dawson. Redding grew up in Macon, where he was influenced by Little Richard and Sam Cooke. Two of his biggest hits were "Try a Little Tenderness" and "(Sittin' on) The Dock of the Bay." He was killed in a plane crash in 1967.

Another famous Georgia R&B and soul performer is Atlanta native Gladys Knight, who recorded the 1973 classic "Midnight Train to Georgia" with her backup singers, the Pips. And beach music lovers still remember the 1960s group The Tams for "What Kind of Fool (Do You Think I Am)." Joseph and Charles Pope, Robert Lee Smith, and Horace Kay formed the group in Atlanta in the 1950s and were joined later by Floyd Ashton.

One of the newest stars in rhythm-and-blues is Usher, who was born Usher Raymond in Chattanooga, Tennessee, in 1978 but moved to Atlanta with his mother in 1990. He has sold millions of albums since signing with LaFace Records. His debut album was the self-titled *Usher.*

Swing

Johnny Mercer of Savannah was one of the most famous songwriters during the "swing" period of Big Band music. Mercer wrote more than 1,000 songs, many of them for Hollywood movies. He won Academy Awards for "Moon River," "Days of Wine and Roses," "In the Cool, Cool, Cool of the

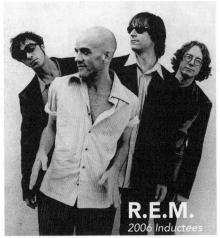

R.E.M.
2006 Inductees

Left: *The B-52s*
Above: *R.E.M.*
GEORGIA MUSIC HALL OF FAME

Evening," and "On the Atchison, Topeka, and the Santa Fe."

Lena Horne was born in Brooklyn, but the famous singer and actress spent part of her childhood in Fort Valley and Atlanta. Best known for the 1943 song and film *Stormy Weather*, Horne performed in other films and Broadway musicals and was active in the civil-rights movement.

Harry James, one of the top trumpet players and Big Band leaders of the '30s and '40s, was born in Albany in 1916. He appeared in several Hollywood films and was married to the actress Betty Grable.

Joe Williams, a jazz vocalist born in Cordele in 1918, performed with Count Basie, Lionel Hampton, and Earl Hines and won several awards as a solo artist. Later in his career, he appeared on television in *The Cosby Show* as Claire Huxtable's father.

Rock and Pop

Phil Walden's Capricorn Records in Macon was responsible for introducing Southern rock music when he signed the Allman Brothers Band in 1969. Chuck Leavell, a pianist and keyboard player with the band, later performed with the Rolling Stones and Eric Clapton. In 1972, a group of musicians in Doraville formed the Atlanta Rhythm Section and continued the tradition of Southern rock.

In the 1970s and early 1980s, Athens was the birthplace of three popular bands: the B-52s, R.E.M., and Widespread Panic.

The women of the B-52s sported beehive hairdos, and the band dressed in funky outfits. One of its biggest hits was "Love Shack."

R.E.M., one of the most critically acclaimed rock bands in the country, was formed in 1980 when University of Georgia student Michael Stipe got together with Peter Buck, Mike Mills, and Bill Berry to rehearse at an abandoned church in Athens. The rest is history. The Grammy Award–winning group has sold more than 70 million records, including the hit single "Losing My Religion." Drummer Bill Berry left R.E.M. in 1995 after suffering a brain aneurysm onstage.

Widespread Panic was formed in 1982 by University of Georgia students John Bell and Mike Houser. They later added bassist Dave Schools and began recording music that was a blend of jazz, Southern rock, and blues.

In the late 1980s in Atlanta, Amy Ray and Emily Saliers formed a pop-rock duo called the Indigo Girls. After gaining national prominence in 1989 with their self-titled album, "Indigo Girls," they won a Grammy in 1990.

Rap and Hip-Hop

Atlanta has become what some consider the new Motown because of its booming rhythm-and-blues, hip-hop, and rap recording industry. One of the first studios was LaFace Records, founded by Antonio "L.A." Reid and Kenneth "Babyface" Edmonds in New York but later relocated to Atlanta. LaFace has recorded artists such as Usher, OutKast, TLC, and Toni Braxton.

Jermaine Dupri added to Atlanta's reputation as a music town when he formed So So Def Records in 1992 after writing and producing songs for the rap group Kriss Kross. He signed the Atlanta group Jagged Edge in 1998 and rapper Lil' Bow Wow in 2000.

Visual Arts

When it comes to men and women who produce fine art, Georgia has very few who are nationally known.

Lamar Dodd (1909–1996), who was head of the University of Georgia Art Department, is considered the state's most influential artist. Dodd's paintings explore both outer space and inner space. In 1963, he began a series of impressionist paintings of the moon, the sun, and the universe. In the 1970s, he looked inward to produce paintings of the human heart. Later, he returned to landscapes, then began painting more violent contemporary subjects, such as the bloody glove from O. J. Simpson's murder trial.

Benny Andrews (1930–2006) was another Georgia artist with a national reputation. The brother of writer Raymond Andrews, he grew up in rural Morgan County, studied at the Art Institute of Chicago, and settled in New York. Even in the North, Andrews's childhood memories influenced most of his work. Using collages, Andrews created expressionistic three-dimensional works depicting different elements of African-American life. After receiving a John Hay Whitney Fellowship in 1965, Andrews returned to Georgia, where he created his *Autobiographical Series*. His works have been exhibited in New York, Philadelphia, and other major cities. In 1969, he cofounded the Black Emergency Cultural Coalition to help get recognition for minority artists.

Although some Georgians collect fine art and appreciate traveling exhibitions of the Great Masters of Europe, more of us are fans and collectors of folk art, or art created by self-taught artists.

The most famous folk artist in Georgia is the late Howard Finster (1915–2001), a Baptist minister who was working at a bicycle shop in Pennville

Elvis *by Howard Finster*
COURTESY OF MORRIS MUSEUM OF ART

when he reported having a vision. In response to the vision, he began creating Paradise Garden, an outdoor collection of sculptures made from plywood, concrete, and bicycle parts. Some were humorous, while others had religious themes. In 1976, he was painting a bicycle when he saw a face in the paint on his fingertip. That was a sign, he believed, to begin painting sacred art. And he did, producing thousands of paintings and becoming famous enough to be invited on Johnny Carson's *Tonight Show*. He later worked with the rock group R.E.M. on album covers. Some of his work is on permanent display at the High Museum

Pasaquan *in Maron County*
GEORGIA DEPARTMENT OF ECONOMIC DEVELOPMENT

of Art in Atlanta. And his Paradise Garden is still open to tourists.

St. EOM (1908–1986), born Eddie Owens Martin, was another self-taught artist in the visionary style of Finster. Martin was the creator of Pasaquan, a series of buildings in Maron County painted inside and out with vividly colored human figures and natural images. Martin began his project after he had visions of futuristic messengers from a place called Pasaquan. The messengers told him to paint a peaceful future for the world. Calling himself St. EOM, he began the art site in 1955 with a 19th-century farmhouse and other buildings on a seven-acre site. Though Martin committed suicide in 1986, Pasaquan remains open to the public. His work is on display at the High Museum of Art in Atlanta and the Albany Museum of Art.

Nellie Mae Rowe (1905–1982) was an African-American folk artist who achieved a national reputation for her colorful drawings in crayon, her sculptures made of dried chewing gum, her plastic flowers, and her works using recycled objects such as egg cartons. Her work can be seen at the Morris Museum of Art in Augusta and the High Museum of Art in Atlanta.

Art Museums

The **Albany Museum of Art** (www.albanymuseum.com) features one of the largest collections of African art in the South.

Brenau University Galleries (www.brenau.edu/discover/galleries), located on the campus of Brenau University in Gainesville, has a permanent collection that includes works by William Merritt Chase, Jasper Johns, Renoir, Cezanne, and Delacroix.

Clark Atlanta University Art Galleries (http://www.cau.edu/art_gallery/art_gal_dir.html) has a large collection of art by African-Americans.

The **Columbus Museum** (www.columbusmuseum.com) focuses on fine and decorative art by artists such as Gilbert Stuart, Robert Rauschenberg, Lamar Dodd, and Benny Andrews.

The **Georgia Museum of Art** (www.uga.edu/gamuseum/) at the University of Georgia is the official museum of the state. The permanent collection includes Italian Renaissance paintings and American paintings by artists such as Georgia O'Keeffe, Winslow Homer, and Jacob Lawrence.

The **High Museum of Art** (www.high.org) in Atlanta has a permanent collection of works by American artists, decorative arts, European paintings, photography, African art, and folk art. Other exhibitions have included the impressionists and works from the Louvre.

Lamar Dodd Art Center (www.Lagrange.edu/academics/art/Lamar-Dodd.htm) at LaGrange College features a permanent exhibit of Dodd's work, as well as American Indian art and 20th-century photography.

Marietta/Cobb Museum of Art (www.Mariettacobbartmuseum.org) features 19th- and 20th-century American art. Exhibitions have included works by regional artists, Winslow Homer, and the Wyeth family.

The **Michael C. Carlos Museum** (www.carlos.emory.edu) at Emory University in Atlanta has an extensive collection of art and artifacts from the ancient world. In addition to objects from Egypt, Greece, and Rome, the museum exhibits works from Asia and sub-Saharan Africa.

The **Morris Museum of Art** (www.Themorris.org) in Augusta opened in 1992. Its primary focus is Southern art. Paintings from the antebellum period to the present provide a visual history of art in the South. Exhibits include works by Benny Andrews, Lamar Dodd, Nellie Mae Rowe, Jasper Johns, and Henry Ossawa Tanner.

The **Museum of Contemporary Art of Georgia** (www.mocaga.org), located in Atlanta, houses works created by artists who were born in Georgia or who moved to the state. Featured artists include Benny Andrews, Radcliffe Bailey, Howard Finster, and Nellie Mae Rowe.

The **Oglethorpe University Museum of Art** (http://museum.oglethorpe.edu/) in Atlanta has

The Preacher *by Benny Andrews*
COURTESY OF THE MORRIS MUSEUM OF ART

hosted exhibitions of works from Spain, Venice, South Africa, and China. "Mystical Arts of Tibet Featuring Personal Sacred Objects of the Dalai Lama" opened here for the 1996 Olympics.

The **Quinlan Visual Arts Center** (www.quinlanartscenter.org) in Gainesville houses a permanent collection of works by local and internationally known artists. Featured artists include Ed and Lamar Dodd, Dennis Campay, Geoffrey Johnson, and Roseta Santiago.

The **Spelman College Museum of Fine Art** (www.spelman.edu/museum/index.shtml) in Atlanta has exhibits focusing primarily on contemporary African and African-American works by women.

The **Telfair Museum of Art** (www.Telfair.org) in Savannah has a permanent collection that includes American impressionist paintings by George Bellows, Robert Henri, and Childe Hassam. It also has an exhibit of 19th-century decorative arts and neoclassical furniture.

The **Tubman African American Museum** (www.Tubmanmuseum.com) in Macon features an extensive collection of African-American art and artifacts. One of the showcased paintings is *From Africa to America*, a mural by Macon artist Wilfred Shroud that depicts important events in African-American history.

Craft Arts

Early Georgians began crafting objects from wood, clay, and fiber for reasons of necessity rather than art. Pottery was used for milk and water containers; quilts and bedspreads were crafted for warmth; wooden baskets and tools were made for use on the farm. As these craftsmen and craftswomen honed their workmanship, they began to create more artistic designs.

The Civil War forced many families who bought these items from factories to return to making their own. After the war, many Georgians, particularly in the mountains in the northern part of the state, began selling handcrafted items for profit.

Today, travelers on the Georgia backroads are likely to find quilts, chenille bedspreads, wooden toys, and pottery for sale at markets and roadside stands.

Fiber Crafts

Georgians have practiced spinning and weaving since the early 1800s. Rural folk and even some of the wealthier Georgians wore homespun clothing made from flax, wool, and cotton. They made dyes from walnuts, red clay, and plants such as indigo, which produced a deep blue color. The art is still practiced today by members of the Chattahoochee Handweavers Guild and other organizations.

Quilting is more popular than ever, thanks to community quilting bees, quilting clubs, and classes. Two of Georgia's most famous quilters were former slave Harriet Powers of Athens and Talula Gilbert Bottoms of Fayette County. Many of Powers's quilts were designed around Bible stories.

In the 1890s, Catherine Evans Whitener of Dalton popularized the technique of tufting cotton sheeting with designs of thick yarn. In French, *chenille* means "caterpillar." Displays of chenille bedspreads were once a familiar sight along U.S. 41. Such bedspreads still can be found in stores around Dalton.

Pottery

Pieces of Georgia pottery, once created for practical uses around the farm, are now works of art selling for hundreds of dollars. The Meaders family was the first to capitalize on the market of tourists and collectors by creating colorful, artistic pieces. Lanier Meaders (1917–1998) of Cleveland improved on his parents' process and began creating jugs with faces. Members of the family still carry on the tradition today. Other folk potters are Michael and Melvin Crocker of Lula and Linda Craven Tolbert of Cleveland. For examples of the many kinds of Georgia pottery, visit the Folk Pottery Museum (www. Folkpotterymuseum.com) in Sautee Nacoochee.

Cleater Meaders making pottery
GEORGIA DEPARTMENT OF ECONOMIC DEVELOPMENT

Wood

Basket weaving is an art still practiced in many parts of Georgia. In the mountains, craftsmen use split white-oak strips as their weaving material. Along the coast, some weavers continue the tradition of the rice plantation slaves by using grasses. Others follow the example of Mrs. M. J. McAfee of West Point and use pine needles. Still others use honeysuckle vines or willow branches.

Various items carved from wood can be found at craft fairs and markets. One of the most popular is the walking stick. On the coast, carvers Arthur "Pete" Dilbert of Savannah and James Cooper of Yamacraw were influenced by the African-American tradition of carving figures of reptiles and human faces into canes.

Drama

Nearly every large city and many small towns in Georgia have community theaters.

Atlanta is the home of the Alliance Theatre, the largest regional theater in the Southeast. Several plays that debuted at the Alliance have gone on to be performed on Broadway. These include *Driving Miss Daisy* by Alfred Uhry, a musical version of Alice Walker's *The Color Purple*, and *Elaborate Lives: The Legend of Aida*, a musical by Elton John and Tim Rice that later won four Tony Awards. Touring Broadway shows also come to town on a regular basis at the historic Fox Theatre and other venues.

The official state folklife play is *Swamp Gravy*, performed from July to October in Colquitt. Cowritten by Joy Jinks and Richard Owen Geer, *Swamp Gravy* was named after a southwestern Georgia soup made from onions, tomatoes, potatoes, and drippings left over from fried fish. The play is a multiracial musical based on stories by and about residents of Miller County. Each year, new stories are added.

Other communities, inspired by *Swamp Gravy*, have begun producing their own folk plays. In 2007, the Sautee Nacoochee Community Association in the North Georgia town of Sautee used local actors to perform stories about the region in *Headwaters: Stories from a Goodly Portion of Beautiful Northeast Georgia*. The next year, the folklife play *Land of Spirit* premiered in Lavonia. The play is made up of true stories about the people and places of northeastern Georgia. In South Georgia, the community of Lyons sponsors *Tales from the Altamaha* during the Vidalia Onion Festival each spring. The

"Swamp Gravy"
GEORGIA DEPARTMENT OF ECONOMIC DEVELOPMENT

production is based on stories by the late colonel T. Ross Sharpe, an author of local color and humor. Plays such as *Swamp Gravy, Headwaters, Land of Spirit, Tales from the Altamaha,* the Social Circle Theater's *Stories from the Well,* and coastal Camden County's *Crooked Rivers* not only entertain, they reveal bits of history about the communities. *Crooked Rivers,* for example, focuses on fishermen, farmers, and the people living and working on the rivers of the coast.

The previously mentioned plays are relatively new, but some performances have been around so long they are traditions. *Heaven Bound* is a popular African-American folk drama featuring spirituals by a black choir. The play premiered at Big Bethel African Methodist Episcopal Church in Atlanta in 1930 and toured the South during the Great Depression. The story depicts a group of black pilgrims on a journey to heaven. Satan leads them astray before clashing with a pilgrim at the end. *Heaven Bound* still plays to packed audiences every year.

Cotton Patch Gospel is another popular musical that is performed regularly. It is based on Southern Baptist minister Clarence Jordan's folksy version of the Gospels of Matthew and John. Atlanta actor Tom Key and stage director Russell Treyz wrote the music in collaboration with songwriter Harry Chapin. In the play, the mother of Jesus is Mary Hagler, daughter of a Baptist deacon. Jesus is born in an abandoned trailer behind Dixie Delite Motor Lodge during Mary and Joseph's trip to Atlanta for an income-tax audit. Instead of being crucified, Jesus is lynched by the Ku Klux Klan after being sentenced by Georgia governor Pilate.

Literature

Georgia does not have the literary heritage of Mississippi or North Carolina, but it has produced more than its share of famous writers. Few people in the country—or the world, for that matter—have not heard of Margaret Mitchell and *Gone With the Wind*. And any reader who loves Southern literature is familiar with Flannery O'Connor, Erskine Caldwell, Carson McCullers, James Dickey, and Pat Conroy.

Our former president, Jimmy Carter, has written several books—including his memoir, *An Hour Before Daylight*, and a historical novel, *The Hornet's Nest*—that are not only entertaining but also informative about life in Georgia from the Revolutionary War to the present.

In addition to homegrown talent, Georgia has become a magnet for writers from other states and countries. Ha Jin, who was born in China, wrote some of his best novels while teaching at Emory University. Now, Salman Rushdie, the author of the controversial novel *The Satanic Verses*, is a visiting professor at Emory.

The following are some of the state's major writers, living and dead, whose work will better acquaint you with what life used to be like in Georgia and what it's like now. These are not all of our important writers, by any means. It would take an entire book to include everyone. But this list is a good place to start. Ask your local librarian or bookseller for other recommendations.

Conrad Aiken (1889–1973): A former poet laureate of Georgia, Aiken was one of the country's major literary figures. He received a Pulitzer Prize for *Selected Poems* (1929) and a National Book Award for *Collected Poems* (1953). Born in Savannah, Aiken lived through a nightmare that greatly affected his personal and literary life. His father, a prominent doctor, shot and killed his wife and then killed himself. Aiken describes his psychological trauma and offers insights about his literary odyssey in his autobiography, *Ushant* (1952).

Raymond Andrews (1934–1991): The son of sharecropper parents, Andrews was the author of several critically acclaimed novels about African-American life in Georgia. His debut novel, *Appalachee Red*, won the James Baldwin Prize for fiction in 1979. Andrews was born in the community of Plainview near Madison. His *Muskhogean* trilogy chronicles black life in the South between World War I and the 1960s. The first of the series, *Appalachee Red*, was followed by *Rosiebelle Lee Wildcat Tennessee* (1980) and *Baby Sweet's* (1963). Andrews's memoir, *The Last Radio Days* (1990), describes his childhood with his black grandmother and white grandfather.

Tina McElroy Ansa (1949–): Ansa, a former journalist for the *Atlanta Constitution*, has staked out her native Macon as the setting for her fictional town of Mulberry. The supernatural elements of African-American life are a common thread in her novels. In her debut novel, *Baby of the Family* (1989), a child is born with a caul, or membrane, covering her head. According to folklore, such a child is endowed with the ability to see ghosts. Her other novels are *Ugly Ways* (1993), *The Hand I Fan With* (1996), and *You Know Better* (2002).

Vereen Bell (1911–1944): A native of Cairo, Georgia, Bell had just begun a successful literary career when he was killed in action in World War II. He wrote a number of stories and magazine articles, but his best-known work is *Swamp Water* (1940), a novel set in the Okefenokee. This story of a young man's friendship with a fugitive was the basis for a 1942 Hollywood film. His other novel, *Two of a Kind* (1943), was serialized in the *Saturday Evening Post*.

Roy Blount, Jr. (1941–): Blount is a Decatur native who has a national reputation as an author and humorist who can explain the oddities of the South to folks who don't live here. He is the author of *Crackers: This Whole Many-Angled Thing of Jimmy, More Carters, Ominous Little Animals, Sad-Singing Women, My Daddy and Me* (1980) and a memoir, *Be Sweet: A Conditional Love Story* (1998). Blount is also a national magazine columnist and a regular guest on the radio show *A Prairie Home Companion*.

David Bottoms (1949–): The current poet laureate of Georgia, Bottoms is a writer whose works often deal with death, nature, and religion in the South. Born in Canton, Bottoms began writing poems at an early age. At 29, he won the 1979 Walt Whitman Award of the Academy of American Poets for his collection *Shooting Rats at the Bibb County Dump* (1980). His other notable poetry collections include *In a U-Haul North of Damascus* (1983) and *Vagrant Grace* (1999).

Olive Ann Burns (1924–1990): Burns, a native of Banks County, did not take fiction writing seriously until she was diagnosed with cancer in 1975. Previously, she had worked as a staff writer and columnist for the *Atlanta Journal and Constitution*'s Sunday magazine, but she quit to raise a family after she married fellow journalist Andrew Sparks. Drawing on her family's history, she wrote *Cold Sassy Tree* (1984), the coming-of-age story of a young boy whose grandfather shocks everyone by remarrying three weeks after his wife dies. The sequel, *Leaving Cold Sassy*, was published posthumously in 1992.

Erskine Caldwell (1903–1987): Caldwell is one of Georgia's greatest writers, although some Southerners have never forgiven him for *Tobacco*

Road (1932) and *God's Little Acre* (1933), novels sharply critical of race and class and controversial because of their sexual content. Even so, some critics have declared *Tobacco Road* one of the 100 most significant novels of the 20th century. During his career, Caldwell produced 25 novels, 12 nonfiction books, and numerous short stories. One of his most important nonfiction books was *You Have Seen Their Faces* (1937), a portrait of country people during the Depression; Caldwell's vivid writing accompanied Margaret Bourke-White's photographs. Born in Coweta County, Caldwell was the son of a schoolteacher and an Associate Reformed Presbyterian minister. His father's passion for social reform was a major influence. Caldwell's autobiography, *With All My Might*, was published shortly before his death in 1987.

Brainard Cheney (1900–1990): Cheney was a member of an elite group of writers that included Flannery O'Connor, Robert Penn Warren, Caroline Gordon, Alan Tate, and Andrew Lytle. Born in Fitzgerald, Cheney attended Vanderbilt University, where he became friends with the Fugitive and Agrarian writers. His novels—*Lightwood* (1939), *River Rogue* (1942), *This Is Adam* (1958), and *Devil's Elbow* (1969)—depict social and racial changes occurring in South Georgia.

Pearl Cleage (1948–): Cleage is an African-American writer whose works deal with civil rights, women's rights, and the black experience. Born in Springfield, Massachusetts, she moved to Atlanta to attend Spelman College. Cleage's debut novel, *What Looks Like Crazy on an Ordinary Day*, was a 1988 Oprah Book Club selection. Her other novels include *I Wish I Had a Red Dress* (2001), *Some Things I Thought I'd Never Do* (2003), and *Babylon Sisters* (2004). One of her best-known nonfiction works is *Mad at Miles: A Black Woman's Guide to Truth* (1990), a criticism of musician Miles Davis's treatment of women and male abusive behavior in general.

Pat Conroy (1945–): Born in Atlanta, Conroy has set most of his works on the South Carolina coast. His memoir *The Water Is Wide* (1972) is about the year he spent teaching black students on Daufuskie Island. *The Great Santini* (1976) is a semi-autobiographical portrait of his father, a United States Marine Corps pilot; *The Lords of Discipline* (1980) is set at his alma mater, the Citadel; and *The Prince of Tides* (1986) and *Beach Music* (1995) both take place mainly in the South Carolina Low Country. All except *Beach Music* have been made into movies. Conroy, who as a student was influenced by the works of Thomas Wolfe, creates a strong sense of place in his fiction while drawing on his personal experiences.

Harry Crews (1935–): A native of Bacon County, Crews has written eloquently about some of the more eccentric characters in the South. His novels include *The Gospel Singer* (1968), *Naked in Garden Hills* (1969),

Car (1972), *The Hawk Is Dying* (1973), *The Gypsy's Curse* (1974), *A Feast of Snakes* (1976), *Scar Lover* (1992), and *An American Family: The Baby with the Curious Markings* (2006). Crews's memoir, *A Childhood: The Biography of a Place* (1978), is a searing portrait of the dangers and hardships of rural life in Georgia in the late '30s and early '40s. In one near-death episode, Crews became ill with a fever that lasted six weeks and caused his legs to draw up severely. In another horrifying incident, he fell into a cast-iron pot of boiling water used to scald hogs and was burned over most of his body. A retired teacher at the University of Florida, Crews was inducted into the Georgia Writers Hall of Fame in 2001.

Janice Daugharty (1944–): Daugharty, who grew up in Echols County, has produced six novels and numerous short stories that reflect the culture and character of South Georgia. Her novels include *Dark of the Moon* (1994), *Necessary Lies* (1995), *Earl in the Yellow Shirt* (1997), and *Like a Sister* (1999). Most of her characters are residents of Cornerville, a fictional South Georgia town.

James Dickey (1928–1997): Dickey is considered one of Georgia's greatest poets, but to most people he is best known as the author of *Deliverance* (1970). The novel and subsequent movie left a lasting—and unflattering—image of Georgia mountain folk. Born in Atlanta, Dickey joined the United States Army Air Corps in 1945 and received five Bronze Stars for his service as a navigator. He honed his skills as a poet while writing advertising copy for McCann-Erickson in Atlanta but eventually quit to teach. In 1968, he became professor and poet-in-residence at the University of South Carolina. Some of Dickey's most memorable poems are "Looking for the Buckhead Boys," "The Sheep Child," "Cherrylog Road," "Firebombing," and "Falling." Dickey was inducted into the Georgia Writers Hall of Fame in 2000.

Berry Fleming (1899–1989): Born in Augusta, Fleming left the South to attend Harvard and to live and write in New York. When he returned home nearly a decade later, he found a true story that would inspire his most popular novel, *Colonel Effingham's Raid* (1943). The story, based on political corruption involving the Cracker Party in Richmond County, was adapted for a film starring Charles Coburn. Some of Fleming's other novels include *Siesta* (1935), *The Lightwood Tree* (1947), *The Winter Rider* (1960), and *The Affair at Honey Hill* (1981).

Melissa Fay Greene (1952–): Greene is a Macon native whose critically acclaimed *Praying for Sheetrock* and *The Temple Bombing* focus on the civil-rights struggle in Georgia and the events that resulted. *Praying for Sheetrock* (1991) is a story of corruption in coastal McIntosh County in the '70s and the clash between white politicians and black activists. *The Temple Bombing*

(1996) is an account of the efforts of Rabbi Jacob Rothschild to bring African-American and white leaders together after his Atlanta temple is bombed and to convince his congregation to support civil rights.

Lewis Grizzard (1946–1994): Grizzard was a popular syndicated humor columnist who defended Southern traditions and wholeheartedly supported the University of Georgia Bulldogs. Born in Fort Benning, Grizzard grew up in Moreland, worked as a sports editor at several newspapers, and began writing a humor column for the *Atlanta Constitution* that was later syndicated in more than 400 publications. His columns and books were always a Southerner's perspective on a changing world. His best-selling books include *Elvis Is Dead and I Don't Feel So Good Myself* (1984) and *Chili Dawgs Always Bark at Night* (1989).

Anthony Grooms (1955–): Tony Grooms is an African-American writer whose work focuses on the effects of the civil-rights movement. His story collection, *Trouble No More* (1995), and his novel, *Bombingham* (2001), each won the Lillian Smith Book Award. In 2006, *Trouble No More*, a collection of stories about history, race, and the black middle class, was selected as the "Book All Georgians Should Read" by the Georgia Center for the Book.

Corra Harris (1869–1935): Although her name is unfamiliar to most Georgians today, Harris was a popular author during the early part of the 20th century. Born in Elbert County, she was a prolific novelist, essayist, and short-story writer whose works appeared in *Harper's* and the *Saturday Evening Post*. The best known of her 19 novels is *A Circuit Rider's Wife* (1910), the story of an itinerant preacher and his wife. The novel inspired the 1951 movie *I'd Climb the Highest Mountain*, which starred Susan Hayward.

Joel Chandler Harris (1845–1908): Harris earned his living as a newspaper editor, but his enduring legacy is his Uncle Remus folk tales. Born in Eatonton, Harris heard many of these stories while working as a printer at Turnwold Plantation and publishing a newspaper called *The Countryman*. After work, Harris would spend time in the slave quarters with Uncle George Terrell, Old Harbert, and Aunt Cissy as they recalled animal stories from Africa. The slave storytellers were inspirations for Uncle Remus and other figures when Harris began writing his tales of Br'er Rabbit and Br'er Fox. He later became associate editor of the *Atlanta Constitution*, working with Henry W. Grady chronicling the emergence of the New South. Harris's first book of African tales, *Uncle Remus: His Songs and His Sayings—The Folklore of the Old Plantation*, was published in 1880 and sold 10,000 copies.

Paul Hemphill (1936–): Born in Birmingham, Alabama, Hemphill is one of Atlanta's most prolific journalists and authors. His subjects include sports, civil rights, country music, and the blue-collar world of truckdrivers. Some of his best-known works are *Long Gone* (1979), *King of the Road* (1989), *Leaving Birmingham* (2000), and *Lovesick Blues* (2005).

Mary Hood (1946–): Hood, a Flannery O'Connor Award winner for her collection of stories *How Far She Went* (1984), writes with a strong sense of the rural communities in both the mountain and coastal areas of Georgia. Born in Brunswick, she lived in a number of counties before settling in Jackson. Hood's second collection of stories, *And Venus Is Blue*, won the Townsend Prize for fiction and the Lillian Smith Award. A recurring theme in Hood's work is the effect urban development has on families and communities. Her first novel, *Familiar Heat*, was published in 1995.

Mac Hyman (1923–1963): Born in Cordele, Hyman was a promising young writer whose life was cut short by a heart attack before his second novel could be published. His debut effort, however, was a tremendous financial and critical success. *No Time for Sergeants* (1954), a story about a clueless farm boy from South Georgia who is drafted into the United States Air Force, became the basis for a television play, a Broadway play, and a film starring Andy Griffith. The international fame he received for *No Time for Sergeants* was so overwhelming that Hyman struggled to complete his second novel. *Take Now Thy Son* was published two years after his death.

Ha Jin (1956–): Ha Jin is the pen name of Xuefei Jin, a Chinese native who served in the army and was educated in China before coming to the United States in 1985. While an assistant professor of poetry at Emory University during the '90s, Ha Jin wrote two volumes of poetry and three short-story collections. *Ocean of Words: Army Stories* (1996) won the PEN/Hemingway Award and *Under the Red Flag* (1997) won the Flannery O'Connor Award for short fiction. The novel *Waiting* (1999) won the National Book Award for fiction and the PEN/Faulkner Award. *War Trash* (2004) also won the PEN/Faulkner Award. His novel *A Free Life* (2007) is the story of an immigrant family that flees to Georgia after the Tiananmen Square massacre. Ha Jin now teaches at Boston University.

Greg Johnson (1953–): Johnson's works focus on issues of the modern South. Born in San Francisco, he moved to Atlanta to earn his doctorate at Emory University. His first novel, *Pagan Babies* (1993), deals with the problems of growing up gay and Catholic in the time of AIDS. In addition to three books of short stories, he has written critical studies of Emily Dickinson and Joyce Carol Oates.

Tayari Jones (1970–): Jones is an African-American short-story writer and novelist whose works focus on Georgia and her hometown of Atlanta. She is a graduate of Spelman College and has a Master of Fine Arts degree from Arizona State University. Jones's best-known novel is *Leaving Atlanta* (2002), a story of three children's lives during the time of the crimes involving missing and murdered children in the late '70s and early '80s. Jones was a fifth-grade student in Atlanta at the time. The book won the Zora Neale Hurston/Richard Wright Foundation Legacy Award for debut fiction. Her second novel, *The Untelling* (2005), a story of a tragedy that disrupts the lives of a black middle-class Atlanta family, won the Lillian Smith Award.

Terry Kay (1938–): Born in Hart County, Kay is a former newspaper journalist and critic who began writing fiction in the mid-1970s after being encouraged by his friend Pat Conroy. His first book, *The Year the Lights Came On* (1976), is a semi-autobiographical novel about Kay's childhood in rural northeastern Georgia. He followed that with *After Eli* (1981), a disturbing tale of an unscrupulous Irishman intent on seducing three women to get a fortune. His next novel, *Dark Thirty* (1984), is a dark tale of violence and revenge. Three of Kay's novels—*To Dance With the White Dog* (1990), *The Runaway* (1997), and *The Valley of Light* (2003)—have been made into Hallmark Hall of Fame television shows. *To Dance With the White Dog,* a mystical story of a widower's friendship with a dog that mysteriously appears shortly after his wife's death, became an international bestseller. Kay was inducted into the Georgia Writers Hall of Fame in 2006.

James Kilgo (1941–2002): Kilgo was a University of Georgia professor known primarily for his collections of essays on hunting, nature, and man's connection to wildlife. *Deep Enough for Ivorybills* (1988) and *An Inheritance of Horses* (1994) both reflected his wonder and appreciation for the natural world. He also wrote fiction. His novel, *Daughter of My People*, won the Townsend Prize for fiction. Born in Darlington, South Carolina, Kilgo spent most of his career at the University of Georgia. Although diagnosed with cancer in 2000, he decided to go on a hunting trip to Africa. His experiences were published shortly after his death in *The Colors of Africa* (2003).

John Oliver Killens (1916–1987): Born in Macon, Killens was an African-American writer whose novels deal with racism and the need for social change. He was a founder of the Harlem Writers Guild in New York in the early 1950s. His first novel, *Youngblood* (1954), is the story of black residents of a fictional Georgia community struggling for their rights during the Depression. His second novel, *And Then We Heard the Thunder* (1963), drew on his experiences as a black serviceman in World War II. Killens received numerous literary awards and was inducted into the Georgia Writers Hall of Fame.

Sidney Lanier (1842–1881): Born in Macon, Lanier was a poet whose works, written during Reconstruction, celebrated the natural world and the landscape of Georgia. His best-known poems include "Corn" (1875), "The Song of the Chattahoochee" (1877), and "The Marshes of Glynn" (1879).

Augustus Baldwin Longstreet (1790–1870): Longstreet was Georgia's first major literary figure. He published *Georgia Scenes, Characters, Incidents, Etc., in the First Half Century of the Republic* in 1835. Born in Augusta, he was a man of many talents. In addition to writing fiction, he was a lawyer, judge, newspaper editor, minister, and college president.

Grace Lumpkin (1891–1980): Lumpkin, a Milledgeville native, was a radical crusader whose novels portray working-class struggles in the South during the Great Depression. *To Make My Bread* (1932) and *A Sign for Cain* (1935) are based on mill strikes in North Carolina and Alabama that erupted into violence.

Carson McCullers (1917–1967): Born in Columbus, McCullers has been ranked among the country's major writers of the 20th century. Loneliness and isolation are recurring themes in her works. *The Heart Is a Lonely Hunter* (1940), *The Ballad of the Sad Café* (1941), *Reflections in a Golden Eye* (1943), and *The Member of the Wedding* (1946) have been adapted for films and Broadway plays. *The Member of the Wedding* ran for 501 performances on Broadway and won the New York Drama Critics Award.

Ralph McGill (1898–1969): As editor and publisher of the *Atlanta Constitution* during the civil-rights movement, McGill was the conscience of the South—a source of hatred for some and an inspiration for others. In his daily column, McGill was a voice of moderation, urging his fellow Southerners to end racial segregation after the 1954 *Brown v. Board of Education* decision by the United States Supreme Court. He was awarded the Pulitzer Prize in 1959 for his columns on the bombing of the Jewish temple in Atlanta. These were reprinted in his book *A Church, a School* (1959). McGill also wrote about his life and the region in *The South and the Southerner* (1963).

James Alan McPherson (1943–): McPherson, a native of Savannah, became the first African-American to win the Pulitzer Prize for fiction when he published *Elbow Room* (1977), a collection of stories. He is the recipient of several prestigious awards, including the MacArthur Fellowship. His other notable works include the story collection *Hue and Cry* (1968) and his memoir, *Crabcakes* (1998).

Caroline Miller (1903–1992): Miller, born in Waycross, became the first Georgian to win the Pulitzer Prize for fiction when she published her novel, *Lamb in His Bosom* (1933). Set in South Georgia during the 19th century, the best-selling novel is the story of a woman's two marriages and her struggle to overcome frontier hardships and the Civil War while giving birth to 14 children. The novel also won France's Prix Femina.

Judson Mitcham (1948–): Mitcham, a native of Monroe, is a poet and novelist who writes about universal human emotions, using rural Georgia

Margaret Mitchell
GEORGIA DEPARTMENT OF ECONOMIC DEVELOPMENT

as a backdrop. One of his best-known poetry collections is *Somewhere in Ecclesiastes* (1991). Mitcham has won the prestigious Townsend Award for fiction twice for his novels *The Sweet Everlasting* (1996) and *Sabbath Creek* (2004). Like his poems, the novels deal with issues of race and class and the influence of an unchanging past on the present.

Margaret Mitchell (1900–1949): Peggy Mitchell of Atlanta published only one book in her lifetime, but what a book it was! *Gone With the Wind* (1936) won the 1937 Pulitzer Prize, introduced one of the most romantic couples in literature, inspired one of the greatest movies of all time, and became one of the best-selling books in the world. Mitchell, who worked for several years as a reporter for the *Atlanta Journal*'s Sunday magazine, began writing the novel to pass the time while recuperating from a broken ankle. Two sequels to *Gone With the Wind* have been penned by other authors, but Mitchell refused to write one herself. Incidentally, Mitchell's famous heroine, Scarlett O'Hara, was initially called Pansy O'Hara.

Flannery O'Connor (1925–1964): A native of Savannah, O'Connor is considered Georgia's greatest writer and one of the best fiction writers in America.

Flannery O'Connor
COURTESY OF GEORGIA ARCHIVES,
VANISHING GEORGIA COLLECTION, BA 1078

Her darkly comic stories often feature eccentric or grotesque characters and are always shadowed by religion (O'Connor was a devout Catholic in the mostly Protestant South). Her best-known works are *A Good Man Is Hard to Find* (1955), *The Violent Bear It Away* (1960), and *Everything That Rises Must Converge* (1965). Stricken with lupus in 1950, O'Connor moved to Milledgeville, where she lived until her death in 1964. Eight years later, *The Complete Stories* received the National Book Award.

Eugenia Price (1916–1996): Price was born in West Virginia but became famous as an author of historical novels after she moved to St. Simons Island. She meticulously researched the history of the Georgia islands to write her fictional *St. Simons* trilogy—*The Beloved Invader* (1965), *New Moon Rising* (1969), and *The Lighthouse* (1971)—and other novels set on the coast.

Janisse Ray (1962–): Ray is an environmentalist and author whose critically acclaimed *Ecology of a Cracker Childhood* is a mix of memoir and ecological message. Born near Baxley in Appling County, Ray was raised in her father's junkyard and barred from watching television. Inspired by her father's love of wildlife, she developed a passion for the vanishing longleaf pines that once forested the area. *Ecology of a Cracker Childhood* (1999) won the Southeastern Booksellers Award for nonfiction and the Southern Book Critics Circle Award. She continued to write about her life and her crusade to save the longleaf pine ecology in *Wild Card Quilt: Taking a Chance on Home* (2003) and *Pinhook: Finding Wholeness in a Fragmented Land* (2005).

Byron Herbert Reece (1917–1958): Reece, born in Union County, was an acclaimed poet and novelist whose brief but brilliant career ended tragically with his suicide. He supported himself by farming and teaching at Young Harris College. His poems, usually on the themes of nature, death, and religion, are written in a lyrical, ballad style. Two of his best collections are *Ballad of the Bones and Other Poems* (1945) and *Bow Down in Jericho* (1950), which was nominated for a Pulitzer Prize.

Ferrol Sams (1922–): Sams—"Sambo" to his friends—had already enjoyed a long career as a physician in Fayette County when he decided to write about his Georgia boyhood. *Run With the Horsemen* (1982), published when he was 60, was the first of his novels featuring protagonist Porter "Sambo" Osborne, Jr. Liberally laced with humor, Sams's novels are an entertaining and accurate portrait of life in rural Georgia before and after World War II. Sams was inducted into the Georgia Writers Hall of Fame in 2007.

Bettie Sellers (1926–): A former poet laureate of Georgia, Sellers lives in Young Harris, where she continues to write about the people of southern Appalachia. Her collections of poetry include *Spring Onions and Cornbread*

(1978), *Morning of the Red-Tailed Hawk* (1981), *Liza's Monday and Other Poems* (1986), and *Wild Ginger* (1989).

Celestine Sibley (1914–1999): Sibley was a journalist and author whose personal columns in the *Atlanta Constitution* revealed as much about Southern culture as they did about her family life. Born in Holley, Florida, Sibley became a columnist after working as a reporter covering some of Georgia's most sensational criminal trials. She also was the author of more than two dozen books, including mystery novels and her memoir, *Turned Funny* (1988), which was adapted into a play. Her novel *Children, My Children* (1982)* won the Townsend Prize for fiction.

Anne Rivers Siddons (1936–): Siddons is a best-selling author of popular fiction usually set in the South. Although she has written about Maine and the South Carolina Low Country in recent years, two of her best-known novels, *Peachtree Road* (1989) and *Downtown* (1994), take place in Atlanta and describe the city's transformation from a "big small town" into a sprawling metropolis. Two other novels, *Homeplace* (1987) and *Nora, Nora* (2000), are set in her hometown of Fairburn.

Lillian Smith (1897–1966): Smith was a white Southern woman who was ahead of her time when it came to civil rights. She was an active foe of racial segregation, a position at the heart of *Strange Fruit* (1944), a story of interracial love, and *Killers of the Dream* (1949). Born in Florida, Smith moved with her family in 1915 to Rabun County, where they started Laurel Falls Girls Camp. Smith later ran the camp and cofounded the liberal magazine *Pseudopodia* with Paula Snelling as a forum open to writers of all races.

Jean Toomer (1894–1967): The son of Georgia parents, Toomer was born in Washington, D.C., and educated in the North, but he found his literary inspiration in the small town of Sparta in Hancock County. While working as a substitute principal, he wrote *Cane* (1923), a narrative of African-American life that encompasses both the North and rural Georgia. Many black writers, including Alice Walker, have acknowledged Toomer's influence on their work.

Alice Walker (1946–): Walker is an African-American novelist and poet whose novel *The Color Purple* (1983) won the Pulitzer Prize and the National Book Award. The daughter of sharecroppers in Eatonton, Walker wrote two novels before her masterpiece was published. *The Color Purple* is a series of letters to God from Celie describing the physical and sexual abuse she endures, her forced marriage, and finally the support she receives from her sister and other women. The book was made into a film by Steven Spielberg in 1985 and was adapted as a musical in 2004.

Bailey White (1950–): White, born in Thomasville, is a former teacher who turned to writing after her National Public Radio essays about eccentric Southerners made her a popular figure. Her essays were collected and published in *Mama Makes Up Her Mind* (1993) and *Sleeping at the Starlite Hotel and Other Adventures on the Way Back Home* (1995). In 1998, she published her first novel, *Quite a Year for Plums*, about a plant pathologist and his romance with a bird artist.

Walter White (1893–1955): Born in Atlanta, White was an author and influential leader of the early civil-rights movement. He founded the Atlanta branch of the National Association for the Advancement of Colored People in 1916 and was the secretary of the NAACP from 1929 to 1955. His novel *Fire in the Flint* (1924) is the story of the lynching of a black doctor. His second novel, *Flight* (1926), is an account of the migration of blacks to the North.

Philip Lee Williams (1950–): Born in Madison, Williams is a prolific author whose works include nine novels, two memoirs, a collection of essays, and a children's book. His first novel, *The Heart of a Distant Forest* (1986), won the Townsend Prize for fiction. It is the story of a professor who goes to a family cabin to die but finds solace in nature and the friendship of a young boy. Williams has written about crime, passionate love affairs, family mysteries, and the environment. Recently, he turned to history for his novel *A Distant Flame* (2004), the story of a Confederate sharpshooter in Atlanta as Union forces attack the city.

Calder Willingham (1922–1995): A native of Atlanta, Willingham is noted for his novel *End As a Man* (1947), based on his experiences as a cadet at the Citadel. Georgia is the setting for *Eternal Fire* (1963) and *Rambling Rose* (1972), which was made into a movie starring Laura Dern, Diane Ladd, and Robert Duvall. Willingham was more famous for his screenwriting talents. He cowrote the screenplays for *The Graduate* and *Little Big Man.*

Frank Yerby (1916–1991): Yerby, born in Augusta, was famous for historical novels such as *The Foxes of Harrow* (1946), which were usually published with suggestive covers. He was the first African-American to write a best-selling novel and to sell the book to Hollywood. He wrote 33 novels that sold more than 55 million copies worldwide. His early novels were set in the antebellum South with white protagonists. In his later life, he began to address racial issues in novels such as *The Serpent and the Staff* (1958) and *Speak Now* (1969).

The Media

The state's first television station, WSB-TV, began broadcasting in 1948. Today, Georgia has 49 or so stations, including nine public television stations under the umbrella of Georgia Public Broadcasting. You can learn a lot about the state by watching shows about Georgia travel, gardening, politics, business, and the arts on public television. Cable News Network (CNN), the worldwide news operation started by Ted Turner, has its headquarters in Atlanta. The Cartoon Network, Turner Classic Movies, and the Weather Channel are also located in the Metro Atlanta area.

Statewide magazines include the business publication *Georgia Trend* and *Georgia Backroads*, which focuses on historical events and travel. Nearly all of the large cities in the state have city magazines. You'll also find specialty magazines on gardening, dining, fashion, social events, weddings, and home décor and regional magazines such as *Points North*, which covers the northern Atlanta suburbs.

The *Atlanta-Journal Constitution* is the largest daily newspaper in the state. Other large papers are located in Columbus, Albany, Augusta, Macon, and Savannah. *Creative Loafing*, an alternative newspaper offering extensive coverage of music and the arts, is available in Atlanta. And the *Atlanta Business Chronicle* is considered an excellent source of local business news.

Books and Resources

Burrison, John A. *Brothers in Clay: The Story of Georgia Folk Pottery*. Athens: University of Georgia Press, 2001.

Georgia Center for the Book. www.georgiacenterforthebook.org.

Georgia Music Hall of Fame. www.georgiamusic.org.

Georgia Writers Hall of Fame. www.libs.edu/gawriters/.

New Georgia Encyclopedia. www.georgiaencyclopedia.org.

Mysteries and Haunted Places

Barnsley Gardens
GEORGIA DEPARTMENT OF ECONOMIC DEVELOPMENT

If you love ghost stories and are fascinated by things that go bump in the night, you'll find plenty to entertain you in Georgia. Savannah is known as "the most haunted city in the country," and other parts of the state have their ghosts and legends as well.

The Pirate's House   It's no wonder that Savannah has so many ghost stories, for it literally was built upon the graves of Native Americans who lived on the site before the first English settlers arrived. Tales of pirates, the Civil War, and crimes of passion embellish Savannah's rich history and have led to the creation of numerous "ghost tours" of the city. One of the most visited spots is the Pirate's House, the site of many drunken brawls in the 18th century and allegedly the tavern where Robert Louis Stevenson wrote parts of *Treasure Island*. Supposedly, Stevenson's Captain Flint died at the Pirate's House while screaming for more rum. No historical record exists that Flint was there, but facts shouldn't get in the way of a good story.

The 17Hundred90 Inn and Restaurant   Two female ghosts—one the spirit of a black cook from the 1850s and the other the spirit of an Irish servant girl named Anna Powers—are believed to haunt this Savannah inn.

The cook's large bracelets can occasionally be heard jangling, and kitchen workers claim to have seen silverware fly off the tables.

Differing stories circulate about Anna. In one version, she threw herself off the third-floor balcony after being abandoned by a sailor she loved. In another, she committed suicide to avoid an arranged marriage to Steel White, the owner of the building. Many of the unusual sights and sounds today are said to take place in Room 204—the very room where Anna was held prisoner in preparation for her wedding.

Juliette Gordon Low House   The Savannah birthplace of the founder of the Girl Scouts of America has attracted both Girl Scouts and ghost hunters. The ghost of Low's father is said to have appeared to escort Low's dying mother to the afterlife. Since then, the staff has reported strange happenings, such as the disappearance and mysterious reappearance of staplers, pens, and other objects.

Barnsley Gardens   This beautiful upscale resort and golf course in northeastern Georgia attracts thousands of visitors and vacationers, but it once was the scene of a series of tragedies. In 1841, Geoffrey Barnsley began building his villa, Woodlands, despite a warning that the land was sacred ground to the Cherokees. While the house was under construction, Barnsley hired famed landscape architect Andrew Jackson Downing to design the elaborate gardens. Before the house was completed, however, Barnsley's wife, Julia, died. As the story goes, Julia's spirit returned to tell Barnsley to finish their home and continued to meet him in the boxwood garden. The subsequent tragic events can be attributed to a Cherokee curse or just plain bad luck. Barnsley suffered severe financial setbacks, his daughter and infant son died, and his oldest son, Howard, was killed by Chinese bandits while on an expedition to find new plants for the garden. During the Civil War, Union soldiers looted Woodlands and drank all the wine in the cellar. Later, Barnsley's son-in-law was killed by a falling tree. In 1906, a tornado tore the roof off the house. One of Barnsley's grandsons, Preston, sustained head injuries as a professional boxer and was institutionalized in the mid-1930s; he escaped after a few months and shot and killed his brother Harry in the living room of Woodlands.

Today, new owners have renovated the house, restored the gardens, and, according to one report, asked two Cherokee chiefs to remove the curse.

Springer Opera House   Luminaries including Oscar Wilde, Ethel Barrymore, and Irving Berlin have appeared at this famous opera house in

Springer Opera House
GEORGIA DEPARTMENT OF ECONOMIC DEVELOPMENT

Columbus since its opening in 1871. But the most famous, Edwin Booth, is still rumored to be hanging around. Booth, determined to restore his reputation after his brother John Wilkes Booth assassinated Abraham Lincoln, toured the country performing *Hamlet*. Years after Booth's appearance at the Springer Opera House, employees reported vanishing props, stage lights that flickered off and on, and other poltergeist happenings. Some say Booth was so thrilled by his reception at the opera house that his spirit returned there.

Strange Lights Everyone is familiar with the natural phenomenon known as the northern lights, but South Georgians claim supernatural phenomena known as "the Cogdell Light" and "the Screven Light."

In Cogdell, a strange light has been sighted frequently near the Okefenokee Swamp. According to one legend, the source is a decapitated railroad man who is searching for his lost head. Another story attributes the light to a slave whose master told him to wait for him with a lantern until he returned from the war. The master never returned, and the slave waited there until he died. Even now, the story goes, his lantern can be seen at a certain crossroads.

The story of the Screven Light is similar to that of the Cogdell Light. In this case, it was a flagman who was killed by a train while swinging his lantern. On certain nights, the light can be seen along the railroad tracks. The light has been attributed to swamp gas, but that hasn't stopped folks from gathering at the tracks hoping to catch a glimpse.

Strange Creatures Georgia has its own versions of Bigfoot and other legendary creatures. One of these is the Wampus Cat, a large feline that allegedly roams the area around Darien on the coast. More than 300 sightings of a snakelike water monster in the Altamaha River have also been reported.

The Georgia Guidestones
GEORGIA DEPARTMENT OF ECONOMIC DEVELOPMENT

And in Winder, a small town near Athens, a creature known as "the Wog" is part of a Creek Indian legend. The beast is described as a longhaired animal the size of a small horse. It has red eyes, long white teeth, and a forked tongue. The Creeks believed the Wog was the devil, who lived in a boiling mud pit. Several sightings of an apelike creature also have been reported in Georgia. Footprints measuring nearly 18 inches long have been found. If you're interested, check out the "Georgia Bigfoot" website, which has details of all the encounters.

Georgia's Stonehenge   Eight miles north of Elberton in northeastern Georgia are six granite slabs standing nearly 20 feet tall and weighing an estimated 100 tons. Known as "the Georgia Guidestones," the slabs are arranged in an astronomical circle and carved with inscriptions in English, Arabic, Hebrew, Russian, Hindi, Chinese, Spanish, and Swahili. The carvings offer admonitions such as "Avoid petty laws and useless officials" and "Be not a cancer on the earth, leave room for nature." The Georgia Guidestones were made nearly three decades ago when an unidentified man walked into the Elberton Granite Finishing Company and said he represented a group of Americans "who seek the age of reason." Using the pseudonym Robert C. Christian, he set up an account with an Elberton bank to finance the project. The identity of Christian has never been revealed.

BOOKS AND RESOURCES

Brown, Alan. *Ghost Hunters of the South.* Jackson: University Press of Mississippi, 2006.

————. *Haunted Georgia: Ghosts and Strange Phenomena of the Peach State.* Mechanicsburg, Pa.: Stackpole Books, 2008.

Cobb, Al. *Savannah's Ghosts.* Whitaker Street Books, 2001.

DeBolt, Margaret Wayt. *Savannah Spectres and Other Strange Tales.* Virginia Beach, Va.: Donning Company, 1984.

Duffey, Barbara. *Banshees, Bugles and Belles: True Ghost Stories of Georgia.* Berryville, Va.: Rockbridge Publishing Company, 1995.

Roberts, Nancy. *Georgia Ghosts.* Winston-Salem, N.C.: John F. Blair, Publisher, 1997.

Turnage, Sheila. *Haunted Inns of the Southeast.* Winston-Salem, N.C.: John F. Blair, Publisher, 2001.

Notable Crimes and Disasters

Centennial Olympic Park in Atlanta, the site of the 1996 Olympics bombing
GEORGIA DEPARTMENT OF ECONOMIC DEVELOPMENT

Georgia has had a number of heinous crimes. One of the most notorious was the case of Leo Frank. In 1913, Frank, a Jewish man in Atlanta, was tried and convicted of raping and murdering Mary Phagan, a 13-year-old girl who worked at the National Pencil Company, where Frank was manager.

Frank was the last person to admit seeing Phagan shortly after she arrived to pick up her $1.20 pay for 12 hours of work. Her bruised and bloodied body was found later that night by a watchman, who called the police. The watchman was initially a suspect, but soon everything—especially public opinion, stirred by anti-Semitism—pointed to Frank as the killer.

The state's main witness was Jim Conley, a black janitor who had been seen washing bloodstains from a shirt. Testifying for the state, he gave four different and contradictory statements about helping Frank dispose of the body.

Frank was convicted. Within days, many influential Jews from the North offered help with his appeals. After all the appeals were exhausted, Georgia governor John Slaton commuted Frank's death sentence to life imprisonment.

Slaton's action angered many and led to the abduction of Frank from his jail cell in Milledgeville by a mob of prominent citizens from Phagan's hometown of Marietta. The men drove Frank back to Marietta and hanged him from an oak tree.

Belated justice was served more than 70 years later when the Georgia State Board of Pardons pardoned Frank. Its decision was based on testimony by Alzonzo Mann, 83, who was an office boy at the pencil factory when he saw Jim Conley carry Mary Phagan's body to the basement. Conley allegedly had threatened to kill Mann if he talked.

The case has been the subject of a television miniseries, *The Murder of Mary Phagan* (1988); a Broadway musical, *Parade*, by Alfred Uhry; and several books. The most recent and most definitive work is *And the Dead Shall Rise: The Murder of Mary Phagan and the Lynching of Leo Frank* by Steve Oney, published in 2003.

Crimes

Atlanta's Missing and Murdered Children From the summer of 1979 until the spring of 1981, Atlantans lived under a cloud of fear and suspicion. During that period, 29 African-American children, teenagers, and adults were killed. Neighbors began to distrust neighbors. Strong rumors circulated that the murders were racially motivated.

In May 1981, police detectives staked out at a bridge over the Chattahoochee River got a break when they heard a splash in the water beneath the structure. A white 1970 station wagon was seen driving away from the bridge. A patrol car and an unmarked vehicle with federal agents followed it. The driver of the car, a young black man named Wayne Williams, was questioned and released. Two days later, the naked body of Nathaniel Cater was found floating a few miles from the bridge where Williams's car had been stopped. Police began collecting fibers and other evidence connected to Williams.

On June 21, 1981, he was arrested and indicted for the deaths of Cater and another victim, Jimmy Ray Payne. On February 27, 1982, Williams was found guilty of the two murders and sentenced to two consecutive life terms in prison. Although some officials speculated that Williams was responsible for other deaths, no one has ever been charged in the remaining cases. Williams, meanwhile, still maintains he is innocent.

Centennial Olympic Park Bombing   The festive atmosphere of the 1996 Olympics in Atlanta was shattered when a bomb exploded in the midst of thousands of spectators at a post-games concert in the park. Two people died as a result of the bombing, and 111 were injured.

Richard Jewell, a security guard who had alerted Georgia Bureau of Investigation officials to a suspicious-looking knapsack, was first hailed as a hero and later scrutinized as "a person of interest." The remains of the knapsack were analyzed and found to have contained nails and three pipe bombs. Other bombings in Atlanta and Birmingham eventually led the FBI to Eric Robert Rudolph as the prime suspect. Despite being the focus of a nationwide manhunt with a $1 million reward, Rudolph disappeared into the Appalachian Mountains for five years. He was arrested on May 31, 2003, in Murphy, North Carolina, and is now serving a life sentence without possibility of parole.

Fulton County Courthouse Shootings   On March 11, 2005, Brian Nichols, who was on trial for rape and false imprisonment, escaped from the Fulton County Courthouse and allegedly went on a killing spree. The Fulton County district attorney's office contends that the following events took place. After overpowering and beating a female deputy, Nichols took her pistol and went to the private chambers of Judge Rowland W. Barnes. Nichols then shot and killed the judge and a female court reporter. As Nichols fled the courthouse, he returned fire on Deputy Sergeant Hoyt Teasley, killing him. Several carjackings later, Nichols allegedly shot and killed United States customs agent David Wilhelm at his home near Lenox Square Mall. Nichols then forced a woman named Ashley Smith into her apartment, where he tied her up. After several hours, Smith convinced Nichols to surrender. Three years later, Nichols was found guilty by a Fulton County jury.

Midnight in the Garden of Good and Evil   The death of a hustler in Savannah and the subsequent four murder trials of a respected art dealer in the 1980s would have remained primarily a local-interest story were it not for a New York author fascinated with the eccentric characters and gothic atmosphere of the coastal city.

Art dealer Jim Williams was accused of killing Danny Hansford, a young man with whom he was suspected of having a sexual relationship. Hansford was shot and killed in a house built by an ancestor of Savannah native and songwriter Johnny Mercer. Williams was finally acquitted eight years later, but by then John Berendt, a former editor of *New York* magazine, had moved to Savannah and begun writing *Midnight in the Garden of Good and Evil* (1994), a book that would forever change the city.

Although the trials are at the heart of the book, Berendt also captures the city and its residents. The real-life characters include the Lady Chablis, a black drag queen and entertainer; pianist Emma Kelly ("the Lady of 6,000 Songs"); Sonny Seiler, Williams's defense attorney and owner of Uga, the University of Georgia's bulldog mascot; and Minerva, a self-described voodoo "root doctor."

The book became an international bestseller that put Savannah on the map as a tourist destination. In 1997, Clint Eastwood's film version premiered in Savannah. It featured Kevin Spacey as Jim Williams and Jude Law as Danny Hansford. The Lady Chablis played herself.

The Woolfolk Murders   On August 6, 1887, Richard and Mattie Woolfolk, their six children, and an elderly female visitor were brutally slain with an ax at their plantation near Macon. The Woolfolks' stepson, Tom, was the only survivor and chief suspect. Although he proclaimed his innocence, blaming the crime on unknown killers, he was tried and hanged on October 29, 1890.

The Alday Family Murders   In a crime with echoes of *In Cold Blood*, Truman Capote's account of the 1959 Clutter family murders in Kansas, six members of the Alday family were shot to death execution-style in 1973 in Donaldsonville. The victims were Ned Alday; his sons Jimmy, Jerry, and Chester; Jerry's wife, Mary; and Ned's brother Aubrey. The murders were cold blooded and random. Carl Isaacs, Wayne Coleman, and George Dungee had escaped from a minimum security prison in Maryland and happened upon the Aldays' mobile home. They broke in and waited as members of the family began arriving separately that afternoon. The three fugitives raped Mary Alday. Isaacs's 15-year-old brother, Billy, accompanied the gang but did not take part in the killings. Carl Isaacs remained on death row until he was executed 30 years later in 2003.

The Mark Barton Killings   In July 1999, Mark Barton, who had lost thousands of dollars as a day-trader in the stock market, opened fire at two Atlanta brokerage firms, killing nine people and injuring 12 others before committing suicide. Later, police discovered the bodies of Barton's wife and two children, who had been bludgeoned to death earlier that week.

Death and the Dentist   In 2006, prominent Gwinnett County dentist Bart Corbin pleaded guilty to killing his wife and a former girlfriend in a case that shocked the Atlanta suburbs. The wife's death appeared at first to be a suicide, but police found similarities to the death of a woman Corbin had dated 14 years earlier. In the best-selling true-crime book *Too Late to Say Goodbye*, author Ann Rule reveals some of the secrets in a troubled marriage that had appeared on the surface to be perfect.

Air Disasters

Two of the worst plane crashes involving Georgians happened half a world apart.

On June 3, 1962, a chartered Boeing 707 carrying many of Atlanta's cultural and civic leaders crashed on takeoff at Orly Field near Paris, France. The 122 victims included members of the Atlanta Art Association returning after a museum tour of Europe. The tragedy was a devastating blow to Atlanta's arts community. In an outpouring of sympathy, millions of dollars were donated to the Atlanta Art Association for the creation of the Memorial Arts Center, later renamed the Woodruff Arts Center.

The second tragic air disaster occurred on April 4, 1977, when a Southern Airways DC-9 jet crashed in the small community of New Hope during a hailstorm. Sixty-eight people were killed and 27 injured. The plane hit a grocery store and several cars before exploding.

Fires

On December 7, 1946, some 120 persons were killed when flames erupted through the 15-story Winecoff Hotel in Atlanta. Of the 160 hotel guests who survived, many were badly burned or suffered fractures when they leaped from windows. The hotel fire remains the worst in the nation's history.

Floods

On November 6, 1977, some 39 people were killed when an earthen dam at Toccoa Falls burst and sent a 30-foot wall of water onto the campus of Toccoa Falls Bible College. Twenty of the victims were children.

Flooding as a result of Tropical Storm Alberto in July 1994 is considered the worst natural disaster in Georgia's recorded history. The storm dumped up to 28 inches of water in some areas. A third of the state's counties were declared federal disaster areas.

Hurricanes

Hurricanes took a heavy toll on life and property in Georgia in the 19th century. On August 27, 1881, some 700 were killed when a storm hit the Georgia coast. More than 1,000 were killed and 30,000 were left homeless when a major hurricane hit the Georgia and South Carolina coasts on August 27 and 28, 1893. And an estimated 179 were killed when a Category 3 hurricane hit Savannah on August 31, 1898. In 1911, a Category 2 hurricane hit Savannah, killing 17 people. The city was hit again in 1940, suffering a death toll of 50.

Hurricane Hugo (1989), Hurricane Bertha (1996), Hurricane Fran (1996), and Hurricane Floyd (1999) caused massive evacuations and property damage in the millions but resulted in no reported deaths.

Tornadoes

The worst tornado disaster in Georgia, and the fifth-deadliest in United States history, occurred in April 1936 when two tornadoes struck Gainesville, killing an estimated 203 people and causing $13 million in property damage.

Nineteen were killed and more than 100 were injured in February 2000 as tornadoes ripped through Camilla in southwestern Georgia.

Education

University of Georgia campus
GEORGIA DEPARTMENT OF ECONOMIC DEVELOPMENT

Georgia became the first state to charter a state-supported university when the general assembly approved the incorporation of the University of Georgia on January 27, 1785. A year earlier, the legislature had set aside 40,000 acres of land as an endowment for an institution of higher learning. Abraham Baldwin, a Connecticut native and Yale University graduate, was elected president of the university at the inaugural meeting of the board of trustees in 1786.

The University of Georgia was officially established in 1801 on 633 acres in northeastern Georgia. Josiah Meigs was named president. The first class graduated in 1804 from the Franklin College of Arts and Sciences. Today, the university offers degrees in agriculture, law, pharmacy, forestry, journalism, veterinary medicine, international affairs, public health, business, environmental sciences, and many other fields.

Other colleges soon followed. In 1931, all of the state-supported institutions of higher learning were placed under the University System of

Georgia, which consists of a board of regents and a chancellor. Each individual institution has its own executive officers.

Founded in 1831, LaGrange College is the oldest private college in Georgia. Located approximately 65 miles southwest of Atlanta, the four-year liberal arts and sciences college is affiliated with the United Methodist Church. In 1833, Baptist-affiliated Mercer College was founded in Macon.

The earliest African-American colleges and universities in Georgia were established immediately following the Civil War. Atlanta University began in 1865, Morehouse College in 1867, Clark College in 1869, and Spelman College in 1881. In 1988, Clark College and Atlanta University merged as Clark Atlanta University. All are separate institutions with separate trustees, faculty, and traditions. Morehouse is for men only, Spelman is for women, and Clark Atlanta is coeducational. Together with Morehouse School of Medicine and the Interdenominational Theological Center, these schools make up the Atlanta University Center, the world's largest consortium of African-American private institutions of higher education.

Students considering higher education in Georgia have an incredible variety of choices. Encompassing 35 colleges and universities, the University System of Georgia is one of the largest public university systems in the country. Two of the schools—the University of Georgia and Georgia Institute of Technology—are among the top 20 public research institutions in the United States. In addition, students can choose among 33 public technical colleges and more than 40 private colleges and universities, including prestigious Emory University and Agnes Scott College.

International students make up a significant percentage of the state's college population. In 2007, more than 19,344 students from 194 countries were enrolled in University System of Georgia institutions.

One of the big advantages of living in Georgia is the HOPE (Helping Outstanding Pupils Educationally) Scholarship. Created during Governor Zell Miller's term, HOPE is a merit-based scholarship funded by the Georgia Lottery. Any student who graduates from a high school in the state with at least a B (3.0) average is eligible for full tuition and fees, plus $300 a year for books, at any public university, college, or technical school in Georgia. The scholarship is renewed every year that the student maintains a B average. The scholarship also pays up to $3,000 for tuition at private schools.

Colleges and Universities

Here is a list of selected Georgia colleges and universities, including brief descriptions and recent information on tuition and enrollment. Tuition figures are for undergraduates for a full academic year, including fees. Out-of-state tuition is included for state-supported institutions. Enrollment figures are for undergraduates. Financial figures are for 2007–2008, according to the *Chronicle of Higher Education*, and are subject to change.

Agnes Scott College   141 East College Avenue, Decatur, Ga. 30030 (404-471-6000; www.agnesscott.edu). Founded in 1899 and affiliated with the Presbyterian Church (U.S.A.), Agnes Scott College is an independent liberal arts college for women. Undergraduate students represent 43 states and 23 countries. Approximately 40 percent study abroad before they graduate. Tuition is $27,387; enrollment is 910.

Albany State University   504 College Drive, Albany, Ga. 31705 (229-430-4600; www.asurams.edu). This historically African-American institution was founded in 1903 as the Albany Bible and Manual Training Institution by Joseph Winthrop Holley to provide religious and industrial education for African-Americans in southwestern Georgia. In 1996, it became Albany State University. It offers seven undergraduate degree programs, including nursing, education, and criminal justice. Tuition is $3,470 for Georgia residents and $12,074 for out-of-state students; enrollment is 3,668.

Atlanta College of Art   1280 Peachtree Street NE, Atlanta, Ga. 30309 (404-733-5001; www.aca.edu/). Established in 1905, the Atlanta College of Art offers courses in art, design, cinematography, photography, computer graphics, and web design. Tuition is $18,400; enrollment is 330.

Atlanta Intercontinental University   6600 Peachtree-Dunwoody Road, 500 Embassy Row, Atlanta, Ga. 30328 (888-379-5888; www.aiuniv.edu/). With campuses in Dunwoody and Buckhead, AICU provides flexible scheduling for students seeking an associate's or bachelor's degree in business, criminal justice, health-care management, design, or information technology. Tuition is $26,386.

Augusta State University   2500 Walton Way, Augusta, Ga. 30904 (800-341-4373; www.aug.edu/). Located in the second-largest city in the state, Augusta State University offers an extensive liberal arts curriculum combined with practical, hands-on experience. Tuition is $3,404 for Georgia residents and $12,008 for out-of-state students.

Berry College P.O. Box 490159, Mount Berry, Ga. 30149 (706-232-5374; www.berry.edu/). Martha Berry founded this private liberal arts college in 1902 for the purpose of giving educational opportunities to rural Georgians. Located near Rome, Berry College offers more than 30 undergraduate majors and dual-degree programs in engineering and medicine in association with the Georgia Institute of Technology and Emory University. Tuition is $20,570; enrollment is 2,008.

Beulah Heights University 892 Berne Street SE, Atlanta, Ga. 30316 (404-627-2681; www.beulah.org/). Beulah Heights is a Bible college offering Bachelor of Arts degrees in biblical education and urban studies. Tuition is $6,530; enrollment is 650.

Brenau University 500 Washington Street SE, Gainesville, Ga. 30501 (770-534-6299; www.brenau.edu/). Brenau is a private liberal arts college for women that also offers coeducational evening, weekend, and online courses. Tuition is $17,700; enrollment is 696.

Brewton-Parker College 201 David-Eliza Fountain Circle, Mount Vernon, Ga. 30445 (912-583-2241; www.bpc.edu/). Founded in 1904, Brewton-Parker is a four-year Christian college affiliated with the Georgia Baptist Convention. It offers five baccalaureate degrees, including Christian studies. Tuition is $14,050; enrollment is 1,050.

Brown-Mackie College 6600 Peachtree-Dunwoody Road NE, Atlanta, Ga. 30328 (770-510-2310; www.brownmackie.edu/). Part of a national chain of colleges, the institution in Atlanta offers five baccalaureate degrees in areas such as criminal justice, business administration, and health care management. Tuition is $9,303.

Carver Bible College 3870 Cascade Road SE, Atlanta, Ga. 30331 (404-527-4520; www.carver.edu/). Carver was established in 1943 to meet the needs of black students seeking an education in theology. It offers Bachelor of Theology and Bachelor of Arts degrees, as well as associate's degrees. Tuition is $6,000.

Clark Atlanta University 223 James P. Brawley Drive SW, Atlanta, Ga. 30314 (404-880-8000; www.cau.edu/). Part of the Atlanta University Center, Clark Atlanta is a predominantly African-American liberal arts institution offering bachelor's and graduate degrees. Tuition is $16,100; enrollment is 3,681.

Clayton State University 2000 Clayton State Boulevard, Morrow, Ga. 30260 (678-466-4000; www.clayton.edu/). *U.S. News & World Report* has ranked Clayton State University as having the most diverse student population among baccalaureate-level colleges and universities in the South. Founded in 1969, the rapidly growing institution is also a pioneer in mobile computing; it was the third public university in the nation to require that each student have access to a notebook computer. Tuition is $3,582 for Georgia residents and $12,186 for out-of-state students; enrollment is 6,000.

Columbus State University 4225 University Avenue, Columbus, Ga. 31907 (706-568-2001; www.colstate.edu/). Founded in 1958 as a junior college, this school became the four-year institution known as Columbus State University in 1965. Columbus State offers more than 50 undergraduate programs and more than 35 master's or specialist's programs ranging from art and premed to criminal justice. Tuition is $3,514 for Georgia residents and $12,118 for out-of-state students; enrollment is 7,224.

Covenant College 14049 Scenic Highway, Lookout Mountain, Ga. 30750 (706-820-1560; www.covenant.edu/). A Presbyterian-affiliated institution with a strong emphasis on theology, Covenant College was founded in Pasadena, California, in 1955 and moved to Lookout Mountain in 1964. Major courses of study include English, business, psychology, education, prelaw, premed, prenursing, and biblical studies. Tuition is $22,830; enrollment is 1,287.

Dalton State College 650 College Drive, Dalton, Ga. 30720 (706-272-4436; www.daltonstate.edu/). Established in 1963, Dalton State College offers a variety of courses in business, education, nursing, technical education, and liberal arts. Tuition is $2,088 for Georgia residents and $7,704 for out-of-state students; enrollment is 4,349.

Emmanuel College 118 Spring Street, Franklin Springs, Ga. 30639 (706-245-7226; www.ec.edu/). Founded in 1919 by the International Pentecostal Holiness Church, Emmanuel College is a private, four-year Christian college with an evangelical foundation. Undergraduate majors include Christian ministries, education, psychology, music, and science. Tuition is $11,566; enrollment is 656.

Emory University 201 Dowman Drive, Atlanta, Ga. 30322 (404-727-6036; www.emory.edu/). Recognized as one of the most prestigious private universities in the country, Emory is home to nine major academic divisions, including professional schools of medicine, theology, law, nursing, public health, and business. Author Salman Rushdie and the Dalai Lama have been among the school's recent visiting professors. Tuition is $34,336; enrollment is 6,646.

Fort Valley State University 1005 State University Drive, Fort Valley, Ga. 31030 (478-825-6211; www.fvsu.edu/). This predominantly African-American university offers bachelor's degrees in more than 50 majors and master's degrees in education and counseling. Tuition is $3,558 for Georgia residents and $12,162 for out-of-state students; enrollment is 2,558.

Georgia College & State University 231 West Hancock Street,

Emory University

Milledgeville, Ga. 31061 (478-445-5004; www.gcsu.edu/). Founded in 1889 as Georgia Normal & Industrial College and later named Georgia College for Women, this school became Georgia College & State University in 1996. It offers more than 36 undergraduate degrees and 25 graduate programs in liberal arts, sciences, business, education, and health sciences. Tuition is $5,066 for Georgia residents and $17,688 for out-of-state students; enrollment is 5,125.

Georgia Gwinnett College 1000 University Center Lane, Lawrenceville, Ga. 30043 (678-407-5000; www.ggc.usg.edu/). In 2005, Gwinnett College became the first new state college created in Georgia since 1970. GGC presently offers a Bachelor of Science degree with majors in biology, psychology, and information technology. It also offers a Bachelor of Business Administration degree. Tuition is $78 per credit hour for Georgia residents and $312 per credit hour for out-of-state students; enrollment is 3,000.

Georgia Institute of Technology 225 North Avenue NW, Atlanta, Ga. 30332 (404-894-2000; www.gatech.edu/). Georgia Tech, as it is popularly known, is one of the top 10 research universities in the nation. Founded in 1885 as a trade school, it has evolved into an institution with majors in engineering, the sciences, and technology. Tuition is $5,642 for Georgia residents and $23,366 for out-of-state students; enrollment is 12,562.

Georgia Southern University P.O. Box 8024, Statesboro, Ga. 30460 (912-681-5611; www.georgiasouthern.edu/). Boasting students from every state in the union and 80 foreign countries, Georgia Southern is one of the most diverse universities in the state. It offers majors in more than 120 areas of study; the Chemistry Department in particular receives high marks. Tuition is $4,082 for Georgia residents and $12,954 for out-of-state students; enrollment is 16,425.

Georgia Southwestern State University 800 Georgia Southwestern University Drive, Americus, Ga. 31709 (800-338-0082; www.gsw.edu/). Founded in 1906, Georgia Southwestern is located near Plains, the hometown of former president Jimmy Carter. The Rosalynn Carter Institute for Caregiving was established in honor of the former first lady. Other programs at the university include the Southwest Georgia Writing Project, the Center for Asian Studies, and the Association for Third World Studies. Tuition is $3,526 for Georgia residents and $12,130 for out-of-state students; enrollment is 2,218.

Georgia State University 33 Gilmer Street, Atlanta, Ga. 30303 (404-413-2000; www.gsu.edu/). Located in downtown Atlanta, Georgia State University originally was intended for commuters and older students. Now that dormitories have been added, the school is focusing on more traditional students. Graduate programs include business, law, education, health and human sciences, and liberal arts. Tuition is $5,484 for Georgia residents and $18,772 for out-of-state students; enrollment is 19,913.

Kennesaw State University 1000 Chastain Road, Kennesaw, Ga. 30144 (770-423-6000; www.Kennesaw.edu/). The third-largest university in Georgia's system, Kennesaw State offers more than 60 bachelor's and master's programs. Nursing students from KSU have one of the highest passing rates on the statewide licensing exam. The executive MBA program in the Coles College of Business is the second largest in the country. Tuition is $3,806 for Georgia residents and $12,678 for out-of-state students; enrollment is 18,269.

LaGrange College 601 Broad Street, LaGrange, Ga. 30240 (706-880-8005; www.lagrange.edu/). Founded in 1831 and affiliated with the United Methodist Church, LaGrange is the oldest private college in Georgia. *U.S. News & World Report* has ranked it among the top 10 comprehensive colleges and considers it one of the "best values" in higher education. Tuition is $18,500; enrollment is 1,091.

Life University 1269 Barclay Circle, Marietta, Ga. 30060 (770-426-2884; www.life.edu/). Life is primarily known for its chiropractic curriculum, but the university also offers courses in business, biology, biopsychology, nutrition, computer information management, and sports health care. Tuition is $7,380; enrollment is 495.

Macon State College 100 College Station Drive, Macon, Ga. 31206 (478-471-2800; www.maconstate.edu/). Founded in 1968 as a junior college,

Macon State has grown into the largest undergraduate college in central Georgia. Tuition is $2,046 for Georgia residents and $7,374 for out-of-state students; enrollment is 6,500.

Mercer University   1400 Coleman Avenue, Macon, Ga. 31207 (478-301-2650; www.mercer.edu/); Atlanta campus: 3001 Mercer University Drive, Atlanta, Ga. 30341 (678-547-6111). This Baptist-affiliated university has 10 colleges and schools, including education, engineering, business and economics, nursing, pharmacy, theology, medicine, and law. Tuition is $28,600; enrollment is 4,213.

Morehouse College   830 Westview Drive, Atlanta, Ga. 30314 (404-681-2800; www.morehouse.edu/). Founded in 1867, Morehouse is the nation's only private historically African-American college for men. Two of its most famous graduates are Martin Luther King, Jr., and film director Spike Lee. Tuition is $19,429; enrollment is 2,800.

North Georgia College & State University   82 College Circle, Dahlonega, Ga. 30597 (706-864-1800; www.ngcsu.edu/). One of six senior military colleges in the United States, North Georgia has produced 36 generals and admirals. Tuition is $3,810 for Georgia residents and $12,414 for out-of-state students; enrollment is 4,595.

Oglethorpe University   4484 Peachtree Road, Atlanta, Ga. 30319 (404-261-1441; www.oglethorpe.edu/). Since 1835, Oglethorpe University has provided a coeducational liberal arts education to a diverse student body. Today, students from 34 states and 31 countries are represented. Tuition is $24,542; enrollment is 1,100.

Paine College   1235 15th Street, Augusta, Ga. 30901 (706-821-8200; www.paine.edu/). Established in 1882, Paine is a private, church-affiliated liberal arts college with a predominantly African-American enrollment. Tuition is $10,694; enrollment is 917.

Piedmont College   165 Central Avenue, Demorest, Ga. 30535 (706-548-8505; www.piedmont.edu/). A small liberal arts college, Piedmont is noted for its "Writing and Speaking Across the Curriculum" program, which requires students to take courses that emphasize written and verbal communication skills. Tuition is $16,500; enrollment is 1,100.

Reinhardt College   7300 Reinhardt College Circle, Waleska, Ga. 30183 (770-720-9191; www.reinhardt.edu/). Founded in 1883, Reinhardt is a private, religious liberal arts college that offers 40 baccalaureate degrees in subjects ranging from business and communication to education and music. Tuition is $14,970; enrollment is 1,028.

Savannah College of Art and Design   P.O. Box 2072, Savannah, Ga. 31402 (912-525-5100; www.scad.edu/); Atlanta campus: 1600 Peachtree

Savannah College of Art and Design
GEORGIA DEPARTMENT OF ECONOMIC DEVELOPMENT

Street, Atlanta, Ga. 30309 (404-253-2700). This private college prepares students for careers in visual and performing arts, architecture, and building and design. Tuition is $24,390; enrollment is 7,521.

Savannah State University   3219 College Street, Savannah, Ga. 31404 (912-356-2181; www.savstate.edu/). Founded in 1890, Savannah State is the oldest public historically black college in Georgia. In addition to traditional courses, it offers environmental and marine science degrees in which students do lab work on the coastal waterways. Tuition is $3,486 for Georgia residents and $10,372 for out-of-state students; enrollment is 3,044.

Shorter College   315 Shorter Avenue, Rome, Ga. 30165 (706-291-2121; www.shorter.edu/). Named Cherokee Baptist Female College when it opened in 1873, this school was renamed Shorter Female College in 1877. The name was changed again when the college began admitting men in the early 1950s. The *Princeton Review* has ranked Shorter as a "Best Value College." Tuition is $15,160; enrollment is 1,040.

South University   709 Mall Boulevard, Savannah, Ga. 31406 (912-201-8000; www.southuniversity.edu/). Established in 1899, South University has campuses in Savannah; Montgomery, Alabama; West Palm Beach and Tampa, Florida; and Columbia, South Carolina. It also offers a wide range of online programs. Tuition is $15,300; enrollment is 963.

Southern Polytechnic State University   1100 South Marietta Parkway, Marietta, Ga. 30060 (678-915-7281; www.spsu.edu/). Founded in 1948, SPSU offers graduate and undergraduate degrees in disciplines ranging from business administration to computer science to software engineering. Tuition is $3,872 for Georgia residents and $13,590 for out-of-state students; enrollment is 4,000.

Spelman College   350 Spelman Lane, Atlanta, Ga. 30314 (404-681-3643; www.spelman.edu/). Consistently ranked among the top liberal arts colleges in the country, Spelman is a private, historically black college for women. Tuition is $18,615; enrollment is 2,290.

Thomas University   1501 Millpond Road, Thomasville, Ga. 31792 (229-226-1621; www.thomas.edu/). Thomas is a small private college offering degrees in business, technology, and education. According to college officials, 94 percent of the graduates find jobs in their fields of study within 90 days of graduation. Tuition is $11,040; enrollment is 800.

Toccoa Falls College   325 Chapel Drive, Toccoa Falls, Ga. 30598 (706-886-6831; www.tfc.edu/). Established in 1907, Toccoa Falls College is an independent coeducational institution with the mission of training men and women for work in Christian ministries and other professions. Tuition is $13,825; enrollment is 925.

Truett-McConnell College   100 Alumni Drive, Cleveland, Ga. 30528 (706-865-2134; www.truett.edu/). After more than a half-century as a two-year college, Truett-McConnell was approved as a four-year institution in 2002. Today, the college offers Bachelor of Arts degrees in music and Christian studies and a Bachelor of Science degree in education with a concentration in early childhood education. Tuition is $13,100; enrollment is 473.

University of Georgia   Terrell Hall, Athens, Ga. 30602 (706-542-8776; www.uga.edu/). Although UGA is famous for its football teams, it is also one of the South's top academic institutions. Since its founding in 1784 as the first state-chartered university in the United States, it has produced 19 Rhodes Scholars. Tuition is $5,622 for Georgia residents and $20,726 for out-of-state students; enrollment is 25,335.

University of West Georgia   1601 Maple Street, Carrollton, Ga. 30118 (678-839-5000; www.westga.edu/). The University of West Georgia has undergone dramatic growth and changes since its beginnings in 1906 as an agricultural and mechanical college. UWG now offers 109 different courses of study, including biology, business, music, and nursing. Tuition is $3,918 for Georgia residents and $12,790 for out-of-state students; enrollment is 8,475.

Valdosta State University   1500 North Patterson Street, Valdosta, Ga. 31698 (229-333-5791; www.valdosta.edu/). This South Georgia university offers students the option of completing their degrees partially online, in work-study programs, or with a year of study abroad. Tuition is $4,038 for Georgia residents and $12,910 for out-of-state students; enrollment is 9,826.

Wesleyan College   4760 Forsyth Road, Macon, Ga. 31204 (800-447-6610; www.wesleyancollege.edu/). Established in 1836 as Georgia Female College, Wesleyan owns the distinction of graduating the first woman in Georgia to receive a medical degree. Tuition is $16,500; enrollment is 600.

University System of Georgia Two-Year Campuses

Abraham Baldwin Agricultural College   2802 Moore Highway, Tifton, Ga. 31793 (229-391-5000; www.abac.edu/).

Atlanta Metropolitan College   1630 Metropolitan Parkway SW, Atlanta, Ga. 30310 (404-756-4000; www.atlm.edu/).

Bainbridge College   2500 East Shotwell Street, Bainbridge, Ga. 39818-0990 (866-825-1715; www.bainbridge.edu/).

Coastal Georgia Community College   3700 Atlanta Avenue, Brunswick, Ga. 31520-3644 (912-264-7235; www.cgcc.edu/).

Darton College   2400 Gillionville Road, Albany, Ga. 31707 (229-317-6000; www.darton.edu/).

East Georgia College   131 College Circle, Swainsboro, Ga. 30401 (478-289-2017; www.ega.edu/); Statesboro campus: 1525-A Fair Road, Statesboro, Ga. 30460.

Gainesville State College   3820 Mundy Mill Road, Oakwood, Ga. 30566 (678-717-3641; www.gc.peachnet.edu/); Oconee campus: 1201 Bishop Farms Parkway, Watkinsville, Ga. 30677.

Georgia Highlands College   415 East Third Avenue at Glenn Milner Boulevard, Rome, Ga. 30161 (800-332-2401; www.highlands.edu/).

Georgia Perimeter College   Office of Admissions, P.O. Box 89000, Atlanta, Ga. 30356 (www.gpc.edu/); Clarkston campus (678-891-3500); Decatur campus (678-891-2470); Dunwoody campus (770-274-5200); Newton campus (770-278-1215).

Gordon College   419 College Drive, Barnesville, Ga. 30204 (770-358-5000; www.gdn.peachnet.edu/).

Middle Georgia College   1100 Second Street SE, Cochran, Ga. 31014 (478-934-6221; www.mgc.edu/).

South Georgia College   100 West College Park Drive, Douglas, Ga. 31533 (912-260-4206; www.sgc.edu/).

Waycross College   2001 South Georgia Parkway, Waycross, Ga. 31503 (912-449-7600; www.waycross.edu/).

Young Harris College   1 College Street, P.O. Box 68, Young Harris, Ga. 30582 (800-241-3754; www.yhc.edu/).

Community Colleges and Technical Schools

Andrew College   501 College Street, Cuthbert, Ga. 39840-5550 (229-732-2171; www.andrewcollege.edu/).

Athens Technical College   800 U.S. 29 North, Athens, Ga. 30601 (706-355-5000; www.athenstech.edu/).

Augusta Technical College   3200 Augusta Tech Drive, Augusta, Ga. 30906 (706-771-4000; www.augustatech.edu/).

Central Georgia Technical College   3300 Macon Tech Drive, Macon, Ga. 31206 (478-757-3400; www.centralgatech.edu/).

Chattahoochee Technical College   980 South Cobb Drive, Marietta, Ga. 30060 (770-528-4545; www.chattcollege.com/).

Columbus Technical College   928 Manchester Expressway, Columbus, Ga. 31904 (706-649-1800; www.columbustech.edu/).

DeKalb Technical College   495 North Indian Creek Drive, Clarkston, Ga. 30021 (404-297-9522; www.dekalbtech.edu/).

Georgia Military College   6280 Bryant Street, Union City, Ga. 30291 (770-306-6400; www.gmc.cc.ga.us).

Griffin Technical College   501 Varsity Road, Griffin, Ga. 30223 (770-228-7348; www.griffintech.edu/).

Gwinnett Technical College   5150 Sugarloaf Parkway, Lawrenceville, Ga. 30043 (770-962-7580; www.gwinnettech.edu/).

Northwestern Technical College   265 Bicentennial Trail, Rock Spring, Ga. 30739 (800-735-5726; www.northwesterntech.edu/).

Savannah Technical College   5717 White Bluff Road, Savannah, Ga. 31405 (912-443-5700; www.savannahtech.edu/).

Southwest Georgia Technical College   15689 U.S. 19 North, Thomasville, Ga. 31792 (229-225-4096; www.southwestgatech.edu/).

West Central Technical College   997 South Ga. 16, Carrollton, Ga. 30116 (770-836-6800; www.westcentraltech.edu/).

Public Schools

Newcomers moving to Georgia with school-age children should contact the school superintendent's office in the county or city school system where they will be living. According to the Georgia Department of Education (www.doe.K12.ga.us), registration is usually held in the spring. Dates vary from system to system, so contact the local school district for specific information. Each school system also has its own calendar of opening and closing days and holidays.

Each school system determines the acceptance of credits and the placement of transfer students from other schools or home study programs. Parents who plan to move to Georgia should consider having their student's current school forward records to the school he or she plans to attend.

Georgia state law requires attendance in a public or private school or a home study program for students from six to 16. The school year includes 180 days of instruction. A child must be six years old on or before September 1 to enter first grade, or five years old before September 1 to enter public kindergarten. Public kindergarten is available but not mandatory. A prekindergarten program for students who are four years old on or before September 1 is offered. School systems require verification of age before enrollment.

Immunizations and Health Records

Before entering a Georgia public school, students must provide certification of eye, ear, and dental examinations. They must use Form 3300 from the Georgia Department of Human Resources at the time of enrollment or within 120 days. Forms are available at public health departments and doctors' offices.

A child entering school for the first time in Georgia, or entering after an absence of more than 12 months in any school year, is required to complete the Form 3231 immunization certificate from the Georgia Department of Human Resources. Immunizations are required for tetanus, measles, polio, hepatitis B, diphtheria, pertussis, mumps, rubella, and chicken pox. Some exceptions on religious or other grounds may be accepted. Check with the local school superintendent's office.

Students entering sixth grade must have two doses of vaccine for measles, mumps, and chicken pox and one dose of Rubella vaccine. More information is available at www.health.state.ga.us/programs/immunization/index.asp.

Testing

All third-grade students are required to pass the Georgia Criterion Referenced Competency Test (CRCT) in reading before they can be promoted to the fourth grade. All fifth-grade students must pass the CRCT in reading and math before they can be promoted to the sixth grade. Students are required to pass standardized assessment tests in the eighth grade before promotion to ninth grade and in the 11th or 12th grade before receiving their diplomas. More information is available through the Georgia Department of Education (www.doe.K12.ga.us).

Homeschooling

Georgia state law for homeschooling requires parents to submit a declaration of their intent to their local school superintendent 30 days after the home study program is established and by September 1 each year after that. The declaration must include names and ages of students, location of the home school, and the dates the parents designate as their school year.

At least 180 days of instruction (four and a half hours daily) are required. Attendance records must be submitted to the superintendent monthly. Parents have to complete annual progress reports and retain them for three years. Parents who teach their children must have at least a high-school diploma or a GED. Private tutors with the same minimum qualifications also can be used. Homeschooled students are required to take a national standardized achievement test every three years, starting at the end of the third grade. The state does not require that parents submit the results to school officials.

For more information, visit www.homeschoolingingeorgia.com.

Motor Vehicle Registration

Georgia highways
GEORGIA DEPARTMENT OF ECONOMIC DEVELOPMENT

The steps you have to take to get a Georgia driver's license depend on your age and previous licensing status.

If you are under 16, you are required to take a 30-hour driver education course. The course is now offered online.

If you have moved to Georgia from another state and need to transfer your license, you have up to 30 days to do so. If you are 18 or older, all you have to do is go to your local driver's license office and present proof of Georgia residency. A current utility bill, rental receipt, bank statement, or letter from an employer will do. You also need to provide your Social Security number, your birth certificate, a valid passport, a military ID card, naturalization papers, or an immigration ID card. You then need to pass an eye examination, surrender your out-of-state license, and pay the required fee.

If you are a teenager with a learner's permit from another state, you must complete an application process. An out-of-state learner's permit is not valid in Georgia.

Newcomers getting license transfers are advised to make an appointment. Otherwise, be prepared to wait in line quite awhile. To make an appointment in the Atlanta area, call 678-413-8500 and choose option three. Others should call 866-754-3687 and choose option three.

Registering Your Vehicle

It's best to get your new Georgia driver's license before attempting to register a car in the state. Georgia law requires drivers to register vehicles within 30 days of purchase or residency and to reapply for a new tag every year. Georgia titles are not required for cars in model years from 1963 to 1985.

The Motor Vehicle Division of the Georgia Department of Revenue takes care of all vehicle titling. Vehicle registrations are administered by the county tax commissioners in the individual counties.

To register your vehicle, you will need a valid Georgia driver's license, a completed title application, a valid out-of-state title, or a manufacturer's certificate of origin for a new car. If you have a lien or lease on the car, you will need to complete an affidavit naming the lienholder. Vehicles that do not have titles must be inspected, and officials must verify that they are not stolen.

Insurance

Other requirements for registration include a successfully completed emissions test and proof of minimum liability insurance. The current requirements are $25,000 per person for bodily injury, $50,000 per accident for bodily injury to two or more persons, and $25,000 for property damage. Your insurance company is required to submit your policy information and vehicle information number electronically to a statewide database. Although police officers can check your insurance status electronically, it's also a good idea to carry a copy of your insurance card or a copy of your policy in your vehicle.

It's important to keep your auto insurance coverage current at all times. If your coverage lapses or your policy is cancelled, you will have to pay a $25 lapse fee and a $60 reinstatement fee before you can renew your tag. Penalties are harsher for repeat offenders. Three-time offenders have their vehicle registrations suspended for six months and must also pay a $25 lapse fee and a $160 reinstatement fee.

Military personnel are exempt from paying auto insurance if they are deployed and their vehicles are not being driven. They can file an affidavit at the local tag office to claim this exemption.

Once you meet all of the above requirements, you still have to pay more fees—$18 for the title and $20 for registration. And yes, you'll also have to pay a fee for your tag. These fees vary depending on the county, so check with your county tax commissioner.

For more information, contact Department of Driver Services, Driver Licensing, P.O. Box 80447, Conyers, Ga. 30013 (866-754-3687 or 678-413-8400; www.dds.ga.gov/) or Title/Registration, Motor Vehicle Division, P.O. Box 740381, Conyers, Ga. 30013 (404-362-6500; www.etax.dor.ga.gov/).

Keeping Your License

In Georgia, as in all other states, driving is a privilege, not a right. Reckless or dangerous drivers can have their licenses suspended for six months or more or even revoked.

Georgia operates on a points system for traffic offenses. If you accumulate 15 points in a two-year period or commit a serious violation, your license will be suspended. Drivers under 21 are subject to having their licenses suspended if they are convicted of a single four-point offense. Points range from one for lane violations to six for excessive speed or illegally passing a stopped school bus.

Anytime your license is suspended or cancelled, count on your automobile insurance premiums to increase. Sometimes, a company will cancel a policy if it considers the driver a future bad risk.

A driver who loses his or her license may be required to take a defensive driving program approved by the Department of Driver Services and pay a reinstatement fee of $210.

For information about getting your license reinstated, call the Department of Driver Services at 866-754-3687 or 678-413-8400.

Emissions Tests

Some counties in Georgia require annual emissions tests for vehicles in the model years from 1984 to 2006. Newer vehicles are exempt, as are models older than 25 years.

If your automobile or light-duty truck is registered in Cherokee, Clayton, Cobb, Coweta, DeKalb, Douglas, Fayette, Forsyth, Fulton, Gwinnett, Henry, Paulding, or Rockdale county, you will have to have its emissions checked. The fee for the test is $25.

Taxes

Some states give residents a break by not levying state income taxes. Unfortunately, Georgia is not one of them. And that's not all the bad news. County governments can charge up to 3 percent local sales tax in addition to Georgia's 4 percent statewide sales tax.

There is some good news if you happen to be 62 or older or totally disabled regardless of age. Beginning on January 1, 2008, retirement income up to $35,000 was made exempt from state income taxes.

Income Tax

Anyone who earns income in Georgia, whether a resident or not, is required to file a state income tax return. Tax forms and booklets are available from the Georgia Department of Revenue and at some libraries and post offices during tax season. The deadline for filing is April 15 or the same date that federal returns are due.

Georgia has six income tax brackets. The rates for single taxpayers are 1 percent for the first $750 of taxable income; 2 percent on incomes between $751 and $2,250; 3 percent on incomes between $2,251 and $3,750; 4 percent on incomes between $3,751 and $5,250; 5 percent on incomes between $5,251 and $7,000; and 6 percent on incomes exceeding $7,000.

Married couples filing joint returns and heads of households pay the same rates, though the brackets tax earnings at 1 percent up to $1,000 and at 6 percent over $10,000.

Georgia residents who pay income taxes to other states are allowed a tax credit.

Some taxpayers whose federal adjusted gross income is $19,999 or less may be eligible for a low-income tax credit.

Sales Tax

You will pay a 4 percent statewide sales tax on most purchases in Georgia, in addition to any local sales tax. Food and prescription drugs are exempt from state sales tax but not from some county sales taxes.

Twice a year, usually in August and October, consumers get a tax holiday for certain purchases. Articles of clothing or footwear costing $100 or less per item are exempt from tax; hair products and accessories such as handbags, jewelry, and watches are not. Personal computers and related accessories costing $1,500 or less and school supplies costing $20 or less are exempt. Exemptions do not apply to items sold at hotels, restaurants, airports, theme parks, and entertainment complexes.

Property Tax

If you own a house, real estate, a motor vehicle, or other personal property, you will have to pay annual taxes. Each county determines what your tax rate, or millage, will be. A tax rate of one mill represents a tax liability of $1 per $1,000 of assessed value. According to the Georgia Department of Revenue, the average county and municipal millage rate is 30 mills, and the state millage rate in each county is .25 mill. Property in Georgia is assessed at 40 percent of the fair market value.

Georgia municipalities also levy property taxes based on assessments by the county and city governments.

Homestead Exemptions

If you are a homeowner, you may be eligible for a homestead exemption from the state of Georgia or from the county in which you own property. To qualify, you must occupy the home as your primary residence. Check with your county tax commissioner for deadlines and requirements.

If you are 65 or older, you can claim an exemption from all state ad valorem taxes and taxes on property up to 10 acres surrounding your home. You also can claim a $4,000 exemption if your income did not exceed $10,000 the previous year. Income from retirement sources and pensions is excluded up to the maximum benefits allowed for an individual and his or her spouse. In 2008, that amount was $52,440.

Disabled veterans and surviving spouses are eligible for a $50,000 exemption from property taxes. The unmarried surviving spouse of a member of the armed forces who was killed or who died as a result of injuries received in a war or other armed conflict can claim a $50,000 exemption as long as he or she does not remarry. And surviving spouses of peace officers and firefighters killed in the line of duty will be granted an exemption for the full value of the homestead as long as they occupy the residence and do not remarry.

Estate Tax

Georgia does not have an inheritance tax or a gift tax. It does have an estate tax. Information about estate taxes and taxes in general is available from the Georgia Department of Revenue, 1800 Century Boulevard NE, Atlanta, GA 30345-3205 (877-602-8477 or 404-417-4477; www.dor.ga.gov).

Index

A.H. Stephens Historic Park, 120
Aaron, Henry "Hank," 7, 79, 82, 113
Aaron, Tommy, 87
Abernathy, Ralph David, 49
Abraham Baldwin Agricultural College, 189
Acworth, Lake, 25
Aerospace and transportation, 73, 74
Aflac, 62
Agnes Scott College, 44, 181
Agribusiness, 69-71
Aiken, Conrad, 155
Albany, 28, 119
Albany Civil Rights Institute, 119
Albany Museum of Art, 149
Albany State University, 181
Alcovy River, 26
Alday family murders, The, 176
Alexander, William, 80
Allatoona, Lake, 25, 97
Allatoona Pass, 97, 98
Allen, Ivan, Jr., 48
Alliance Theatre, 141, 153
Allman Brothers Band, 112, 146
Allman, Duane, 113
Alpharetta, 30
Altamaha River, 23, 32, 114, 170
Alto, 14, 133
Americus, 116, 142
Amicalola Falls, 13, 93
Amicalola Falls State Park, 33, 120
Andalusia Farm, 53, 111
Anderson, Bill, 112, 144
Andersonville National Historic Site, 50, 116
Andersonville Prison, 42
Andrew College, 217
Andrews, Benny, 148, 150
Andrews, James M., 41, 42
Andrews, Raymond, 155
Anna Ruby Falls, 13, 25
Ansa, Tina McElroy, 155, 156
Appalachian Plateau, 11
Appalachian Trail, 13, 93
Apple Festival, 98
Arnall, Ellis, 47, 48
Arp, Bill, 43
Ashburn, 148
Ashton, Floyd, 145
Athens, 13, 28, 40, 66, 105, 106, 142
Athens Technical College, 190
Atlanta, 4, 6, 16, 23, 27, 28, 30, 31, 33, 42, 44, 48, 49, 51, 53, 76, 79, 100-105, 141, 142, 174-76
Atlanta Botanical Garden, 102
Atlanta Braves, 7, 79, 82, 83, 100
Atlanta Business Chronicle, 167
Atlanta College of Art, 181
Atlanta Constitution, 5, 43, 48, 67
Atlanta Cyclorama, 50, 100
Atlanta Dream, 86, 100
Atlanta Falcons, 83, 84, 100

Atlanta Hawks, 84, 85, 100, 102
Atlanta History Center, 53
Atlanta Intercontinental University, 181
Atlanta Journal-Constitution, 7, 90, 142, 165, 167
Atlanta Metropolitan College, 189
Atlanta Motor Speedway, 89
Atlanta Rhythm Section, 146
Atlanta State Farmers Market, 132
Atlanta Symphony Orchestra, 5, 158
Atlanta Thrashers, 85, 100
Atlanta Track Club, 90
Atlanta University, 180
Atlantic Coastal Plain, 11, 13
Auburn Avenue Historic District, 102
Audubon, John James, 20
Augusta, 13, 27, 31, 37, 39, 66, 79, 106, 107, 141, 142
Augusta National Golf Club, 86, 107
Augusta Riverwalk, 106
Augusta State University, 181
Augusta Technical College, 190

B-52s, 147
Babyland General Hospital, 93
Bailey, Radcliffe, 150
Bainbridge College, 189
Baldwin, Abraham, 179
barbecue, 132
Barnes, Rowland W., 175
Barnes, Roy, 49
Barnsley Gardens, 169
Barnsley Gardens Resort, 98
Barnsley, Geoffrey, 98, 169
Barnsley, Julia, 98, 169
barrier islands, 12
Barrymore, Ethel, 169
Barton, Mark, 176
Bartram, John, 20
Basinger, Kim, 8
Battle of Bloody Marsh, 37, 50
Battle of Chickamauga, 44, 99
Baxley, 114
Beatty, Ned, 13
Bell, Griffin, 8
Bell, Vereen, 156
Bellows, George, 151
Belue, Buck, 81
Bendzunas Glass Studio and Gallery, 97
Berendt, John, 75, 108, 176
Berlin, Irving, 194
Berry, Bill, 147
Berry College, 44, 181
Beulah Heights University, 181
Bibb Manufacturing, 68
Bibby, Mike, 85
Big Bethel African Methodist Episcopal Church, 154
Big Pig Jig. *See* Slosheye Trail Big Pig Jig
Big Shanty, 41
Bigfoot, 171
Birds of America, 20
Black Belt, 13